City & Guilds
Level 1 Certificate for IT Users

IT Principles

Level
1

Tina Lawton

City&
Guilds

Heinemann

Heinemann Educational Publishers,
Halley Court, Jordan Hill, Oxford, OX2 8EJ
Part of Harcourt Education

Heinemann is the registered trademark of Harcourt Education Limited

© Tina Lawton, 2002

First published in 2002

2005   2004
10 9 8 7 6 5 4 3

A catalogue record is available for this book from the British Library on request.

ISBN 0 435 46261 X

Typeset by Techset Ltd, Gateshead
Printed and bound in UK by Thomson Litho Ltd

Tel: 01865 888058 www.heinemann.co.uk

Acknowledgements
The publishers wish to thank the following for the use of photos in this book: Epson
(pages 8, 10, 11); Chris Honeywell (page 8, top); Anthony King, Medimage (page 4,
top; page 7, page 24); popperfoto/Toshiy Uki Aizawa/Reuters (page 4, bottom);
Science Photo Library/Colin Cuthbert (page 3).

Contents

Introduction

City and Guilds e-Quals is an exciting new range of IT qualifications developed with leading industry experts. These comprehensive, progressive awards cover everything from getting to grips with basic IT to gaining the latest professional skills.

The range consists of both user and practitioner qualifications. User qualifications (Levels 1–3) are ideal for those who use IT as part of their job or in life generally, while practitioner qualifications (Levels 2–3) have been developed for those who need to boost their professional skills in, for example, networking or software development.

e-Quals boasts on-line testing and a dedicated website with news and support materials and web-based training. The qualifications reflect industry standards and meet the requirements of the National Qualifications Framework.

With e-Quals you will not only develop your expertise, you will gain a qualification that is recognised by employers all over the world.

This unit is all about the basic principles of IT – the building blocks of information that will help you to learn about your computer, and, more importantly, what it can do for you.

It can seem quite a confusing world when you first start to explore the mysteries of IT, but there is such a vast store of exciting and interesting things to discover, that you'll be surprised how quickly time passes as you become absorbed in finding out just what you can achieve. Working through the sections, you will be able to learn about a wide range of topics from software to storage, memory to e-mail, and icons to Internet. You will be able to find out how to keep your equipment in good shape and yourself too!

Throughout the unit there are challenges to test your knowledge and opportunities to 'try it out' for yourself. At the end of the book there's an assignment and a multiple choice test for you to use as a practice to make sure you're absolutely ready to pass the real thing.

Although this book covers the syllabus for the City & Guilds IT Users Level 1 Certificate Unit 001, it would be just as helpful for anyone wanting to learn about IT.

Acknowledgements

My grateful thanks to: Stuart for his constant support and understanding – not to mention the endless cups of tea; Keith and Anna for their advice when I got stuck; Nick, Franny and Brian for helping me out with the network screen dumps; last, but not least, Pen, for believing I could do it.

You will learn to

- Identify the main components of a computer and their uses
  - ☐ Identify and describe the central processing unit
    - – State the purpose of 'volatile' and 'non-volatile' memory
  - ☐ Identify and describe input devices
  - ☐ Identify and describe output devices
  - ☐ Identify different types of printers: laser, colour laser, inkjet, dot matrix
  - ☐ Identify different sizes of: paper, envelopes and labels
  - ☐ Change a printer cartridge
- Identify the use of a modem
- Recognise and report problems

Introduction to information technology

Information technology (IT) is a term used to cover all the different types of technologies involved in processing and transmitting information. These include computers, telephones, fax machines and televisions. This book will focus on how the personal computer (PC) is used in IT.

PCs have changed the way we work, in our jobs and at home. We come across them almost everywhere we go today – from our shopping trips to our leisure time activities; from our desk at work or college to the doctor's surgery. The PC helps us perform very complex tasks quickly and easily and this has resulted in an increasing demand for people with IT skills to keep the wheels of the 'Information Society' turning.

Computers in our lives

In the not so distant past computers were very large machines which filled whole rooms and needed special conditions and technicians to operate them. As computers have got smaller (thanks to microchip technology) they have become faster, more reliable and easier to use. With all these advances came a reduction in the cost of computers. People can now afford to buy them to use at home, not just at the office.

Computers at home

Many of the computers bought for use at home are able to access the Internet, where vast quantities of data and information can be found. Computers are used for a variety of tasks by all the family. These might include:

- keeping track of your money and seeing where it all goes!
- sending e-mails and helping you to keep in touch with people across the world

- writing letters, doing homework, designing posters and newletters
- keeping track of your possessions, such as your CD collection
- composing or recording music to listen to away from the computer
- teleworking, i.e. working from home using your computer to keep you in touch with your office or customers
- surfing the Internet to find out information or to buy goods on-line.
- playing games
- possibly being able in the future to control many of our household appliances.

Computers at work or education

Most businesses and large organisations have used computers to process, analyse and record huge amounts of data since the early 1970s. As computers have become smaller and cheaper, most businesses have come to rely on the speed and efficiency of these machines. They can often do calculations many times faster than we could, and they can store data in many forms which take up far less space than traditional filing cabinets. Some of the uses in business are:

- keeping track of names and addresses, such as on a membership list
- producing the payroll
- maintaining accounts
- keeping control of stock and calculating sales
- writing documents such as letters, memos
- designing and producing posters, brochures, flyers, etc.
- using websites to advertise and sell goods
- creating designs such as car models, gardens
- controlling robots and other automated tasks in manufacturing
- keeping track of student achievement
- using computer tests to assess students' skills
- controlling traffic such as traffic lights and speed cameras
- Computer based training and computer based learning.

There are still some areas, though, where computers can't replace the skills needed, such as in the caring professions – nurses and doctors – and in the case of inventors, designers and communicators.

Try it out!

Either think about what you did last week or keep a log for the next seven days and list all the occasions when you have come into contact with computers directly or indirectly. Coming into contact directly could involve using your computer at work or college to produce a document; indirectly could be when going shopping and paying for your goods at the till using a debit card. You may be able to add more items to the lists above or find some different examples.

Types of computer

Computers come in a variety of shapes and sizes, from huge **mainframe** computers which fill a room to very light and small **laptop** machines. The costs of the different computers can vary from millions of pounds to a few hundred, depending on the components which go together to make up the machine. Whatever their size and shape, they all process, store and transmit information, making the end results meaningful to us by using a digital data processor. Unlike humans who get tired and can make mistakes, computers can repeat the same actions without errors very much quicker than we can.

Super, mainframe and mini

In the 1960s and 1970s the computer was a huge machine which filled a room and needed an army of white-coated technicians to keep it running, but today most **mainframe** computers are much smaller, although they are probably many times more powerful than the giant mainframes of the past. In fact, the power of the computer sitting on your desk at home or at work is probably greater than the mainframe computer of the 1970s. A mainframe computer is now usually called a 'large server' and will

Mainframe computer

have massive processing power and storage capacity. These mainframes will usually have either dumb terminals (keyboard and display unit only) or PCs attached, giving many people access to the speed and processing power of the server.

Even more powerful are the **supercomputers**, which offer more power and speed and can support a large number of networked computers and other peripheral hardware (other items of equipment which can be used with a computer, such as a printer). A supercomputer might be used for weather forecasting, when large numbers of operations need to be completed quickly and accurately.

On the other side of the supercomputers are the **minicomputers** – smaller servers – which are cheaper to buy than mainframes. These are usually called mid-range servers and, more often than not, are used as part of a network. Smaller businesses and research laboratories would use these minicomputers to help them with their work.

Network computers

Many computers in the home are 'standalone' machines, which means they are not connected to another computer, although, increasingly, even home computers are being joined together to make a small network. In a **network**, computers are joined together so that they can share systems, data and peripherals, and they don't even need to be in the same building to do this! Whenever you connect to the Internet via your phone line you are joining a huge network which covers the globe. Small businesses, schools and colleges will often have a network as it means that one printer can be shared amongst several computer users, as well as sharing information and other resources.

Personal computers

This is probably the computer you know already – it is small enough to fit on a desktop and is now cheap enough to be available for use in the home. These computers are sometimes called **microcomputers**. The advances made in computer technology over the last couple of decades have meant that the processor, the 'brains' of the computer, has got faster and more powerful. The Intel Pentium chip is one of the latest in a long line of processors which have brought faster computers to the desktop. There are two types of computer which are commonly used today – the PC (based on the IBM PC from the early 1980s) and the Apple Macintosh. The one we are most familiar with is the PC, used in businesses, schools and colleges, and industry. The Apple Macintosh, known as the Mac, is used in publishing and design and for other creative tasks, as it is better able to use its processing power to handle the large graphic files used in these fields.

A personal computer

Laptop computers

The trend for making computers smaller and more portable continued with the introduction of the **laptop**. As chips were able to hold increasing amounts of circuitry, laptops, notebooks, and eventually palmtops have been introduced. These are much smaller than the desktop PC and can be run on battery power alone for short periods of time. They have a screen incorporated into the case, and will often have CD or DVD-ROM drives included, as well as the keyboard, floppy drive and pointer device. The portability of these machines has meant that business has been able to operate on the move. Train travellers can continue their work as they complete their journeys and people like politicians can access up-to-date information as they travel across the world.

A laptop computer

→ **Check your knowledge 1**

1 Which of the following is not a computer?
   a a laptop
   b a mainframe
   c a fax machine
   d a PC

2 Computers can do some tasks better than humans because:
   a they can repeat tasks without making mistakes
   b they are good inventors
   c they are good listeners
   d they get tired

Components of a computer: Hardware

The **hardware** consists of the parts you can actually touch, hold and move (although this needs to be done carefully to avoid damage). A basic computer system consists of the base unit and other hardware devices which are attached to the computer. These devices are usually called **peripherals** and could include the keyboard, mouse, VDU (Visual Display Unit – often called the screen or monitor), disk drive and printer.

The base unit, which is the main box of the computer system, contains all the computer's electronics and printed circuit boards. It will usually have a floppy disk drive and a CD-ROM drive. The hard disk, which stores all the programs, is fixed inside the unit.

At the back of the unit are all the various ports where you would plug in your peripherals. Many of these ports have different functions and it is important, when setting up your computer, to make sure the peripheral devices are connected to the right port because the computer 'talks' to them through these ports.

The diagram below shows the layout of a typical computer system.

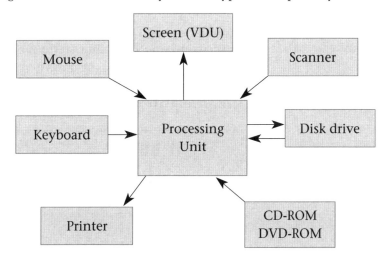

Figure 1.1 A typical computer system

If you look closely at the arrows you can see that they go in different directions – those in Figure 1.1 show the direction of data movement. Data goes from the processor to the screen so we can see the image of our work. The screen is called an **output** device. We use the keyboard to enter data into the processor – this is called an **input** device. Some peripherals have arrows in both directions, such as the disk drive, because data can move from the disk drive to the processor and from the processor to the disk drive. A disk drive is called a **storage** device. Some CD drives (CD-R) are recordable drives as well, and are also storage devices as they can send and receive data.

Central processing unit (CPU)

The **central processing unit** is sometimes called the 'brains' of the computer, as this is where most of the operations are carried out. The CPU can vary from being a single silicon chip (a thin wafer with circuits printed onto it by a photographic process) in a PC to several printed circuit boards in a mainframe computer. The CPU is made up of different parts, each with its own job to do. The **Arithmetic Logic Unit** (ALU) performs all the calculations and logical comparisons. The **control unit** controls movement of data inside the computer, between the computer and the peripheral devices, and the timing of operations. The control unit will send information to the high-speed memory for temporary storage until it is needed.

There are two different types of memory in a computer – **Read Only Memory (ROM)** and **Random Access Memory (RAM)**.

Read Only Memory can't be altered by the user and data in this type of memory isn't lost when the computer is switched off. ROM is used to hold the instructions needed to start up the computer. ROM is called **non-volatile memory**. ROM memory is like the written instructions you read when you want to know how to do something, like following a recipe – you can't re-write the recipe in the book (it's still there when you close the pages!), but you do need to read the instructions before you can start to make your dish.

Random Access Memory needs electricity to keep it going – rather like the food you eat to keep your brain working – without it, your brain wouldn't work! RAM is used to store data about the work you are doing and is the computer's fast short-term memory. It holds information which can be used quickly and easily and then be replaced by other data. As soon as the computer is switched off, the information in the RAM is lost. RAM is called **volatile memory**.

> ### Try it out!
>
> Look up the word **volatile** in a dictionary and see if you can work out why it is used to describe RAM.

Input devices

There are many different input devices, with new devices being invented all the time. Some of the most common are the following.

Keyboard

Keyboards, like the one in the picture below, are used to input data into the computer. If you want to write a letter, you will use the keyboard to type in the words you want to send. The computer will process the signals from the keyboard and change them into recognisable text on the screen. There are many different types and shapes of keyboard, but most of them will have the main keys set out in a layout called QWERTY.

Try it out!

Look carefully at a keyboard and write down the first six letters of the main keys along the top row, going from left to right. What do they spell?

For some people there are specially designed keyboards which can help them to use a computer more easily. These might have larger keys or overlays which can be placed over the keyboard with pictures or colours. There are a number of settings in Microsoft Windows Operating System (more about operating systems later) which can change the way a keyboard works to help people, such as making bleeps when a key is pressed twice to warn the user that they may have made a mistake.

Most keyboards will have other keys, too, which all perform different tasks. Some will allow you to access different programs, whilst others may allow you to do things quickly using a combination of keys. This can sometimes be quicker than using the mouse to perform the same action – these are often called 'hotkeys'. There is more about the keyboard and keyboard functions in Section 4.

Mouse

A mouse is a pointing device which usually has a small ball underneath. As you move the mouse over a flat surface the ball rotates and this sends signals to the computer about the direction of rotation. This is translated to movements on the screen in the form of a cursor or mouse pointer. You can use the mouse to move the cursor on the screen to perform various actions. Most mice have at least two buttons on the top which can be used to select items, start actions and cancel choices.

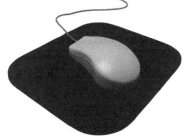

A mouse

Some mice have infrared sensors underneath instead of a ball and others can be used as remote mice. These will send signals to a box connected to the computer which means that you won't have wires getting in the way.

Trackball

A trackball isn't moved around like a mouse, because the ball is on top of the unit – a bit like a mouse on its back! The ball is moved by hand and sends the signals to the computer. Laptops may have trackballs as they take up less space than a mouse.

A trackball

Touchpad

A touchpad is also often used in laptops as they too take up less space. Cursor movements on the screen are controlled by the movements and pressure of fingers over the pad.

Joystick

A joystick is often used to play games. Like a mouse, it is used to input directional information. This information is then used by the computer to control the movement of objects in the game.

Graphics tablet

This is a flat surface on which you can draw using a special pen. As you draw, the movements are detected by the surface and the information is sent to the computer to be translated into lines on the screen. A graphics tablet is used to input freehand drawings into a computer.

Scanner

A scanner is a device which can copy an image or text and send the data to the computer to be stored on a disk or displayed on the screen. Copies can be in black and white or colour and the images produced can be edited on the screen. Most scanners are flatbeds, which look a little like a small photocopier with a glass plate and a lid, but there are smaller handheld scanners which can scan parts of a document.

A scanner

Digital camera

A digital camera can be used to take photographs in a way similar to a conventional camera. The image in a digital camera is in a digital form, and can be inputted into the computer, which then translates the data into the original image which appears on the screen.

Microphones

A microphone can be used when the input is sound, such as speech, and the computer translates the sound into digital data. Speech recognition software will convert the words you are saying into text in a word processing program.

> ### → Check your knowledge 2
>
> 1 RAM is:
>   a memory which isn't lost when the computer is switched off
>   b short-term memory
>   c used to store the programs to start up the computer
>   d non-volatile memory
> 2 Which of the following are not input devices?
>   a mouse
>   b keyboard
>   c scanner
>   d printer
> 3 An input device is used to:
>   a display the data
>   b process data
>   c send data to the computer
>   d receive data from the computer

Output devices

Display screens (VDU)

The display screen is an essential part of a computer to enable you to see what you are doing. These are sometimes referred to as monitors and can give black and white or colour images, although black and white screens are becoming quite rare. Screens come in a range of sizes and types. Until recently, the monitor most often found with a PC had a cathode ray tube (CRT), very similar to the tube in your television, and could be quite large and bulky. Flatter screens are now being used which use either liquid crystal display (LCD) technology, similar to the calculator display, or thin film transistor (TFT) technology. Most laptops will use one or the other of these flatter screens as they take up far less space and are much lighter.

The resolution of a monitor is very important as this will determine the sharpness and clarity of the picture. The higher the resolution, the clearer and sharper the image. The screen image is made up of little squares called pixels (picture elements). The more squares there are, the clearer the image will be. Resolution values are shown in pixels such as 640 x 480 pixels.

Screens are measured across the diagonal of the glass which can be anything from 14 inches to over 20 inches. The larger the screen, the easier it is to read the information, although larger screens can be more expensive.

Speakers

Speakers on a computer are used in much the same way as speakers on a music system. They are attached to the computer by cables or, sometimes, built into the case itself. Music can be played through the speakers, perhaps using the CD-ROM drive to play a music CD, or from music files composed by you or downloaded from the Internet. Most modern PCs will be able to play music and sounds as they will have a sound card installed inside the base unit. The sound card changes the signal from analogue (continuous waves) to the 0s and 1s of digital data, processes it, and turns it back into an analogue signal which we can hear through the speakers.

With special software, speakers can play back what has been typed into a word processing system and allow the typist to hear if the right words have been used.

Printers

The choice of printer will depend on the tasks you will want it to do. You need to think about the speed of printing, the volume (how many copies you will want), whether you want black and white or colour, and the quality of the printed copy.

Inkjet printers

Many home computers have **inkjet printers** because they are relatively cheap to buy and will produce colour prints of a reasonable quality. They can be expensive to run as the cartridges have to be replaced quite frequently and can be costly. Inkjet printers produce their image by spraying tiny drops of ink onto the paper. They make up an image from the dots and the higher the number of **dots per inch** (dpi), the higher the quality of the output. Inkjets printers are able to handle different media such as acetates, envelopes and other specialist paper, as well as A4 printing paper. The quality of the paper is also important as a paper that is very absorbent might not give a clear image.

An inkjet printer

Laser printers

A laser printer uses a laser beam to build up an electrical image of a page on a light sensitive drum in a similar way to a photocopier. The image is built up from dots but there are usually more dots per inch for the lowest quality output than with an inkjet printer. In fact a laser printer can produce an image of 2400 dpi, which will give a very high quality print for both text and graphics. A powder called toner is attracted to the pattern formed on the drum and as the

Laser printer

paper passes through the printer it is held against the drum and heated to fix the powder to the paper. The cartridges which hold the toner are very expensive and have to be replaced occasionally, but laser printers will produce a high volume of quality prints before the cartridge needs replacing. This can make them cheaper for printing black and white than inkjet printers.

Colour laser printers

The **colour laser printer** uses a similar process to the normal laser printers, but instead of just one toner cartridge (black) they need a toner cartridge for each of the four colours used in the printing process. This makes them slower and more expensive to use than inkjet printers, although they will produce top quality prints. They are very expensive to buy, although the prices are continuing to drop as the technology inside them gets cheaper and easier to mass produce.

Dot matrix printers

Dot matrix printers are **impact** printers where patterns of wires called printing pins hit a carbon ribbon in response to signals from the computer. This transfers the pattern onto the paper in the form of characters or graphics. Dot matrix printers tend to be regarded as old technology as they are slow and noisy, with a lower quality output. They are still useful for some tasks though, as they can handle multi-part forms and continuous stationery, and are cheap to buy and run.

Dot matrix printer

Consumables: Paper, envelopes and labels

All printers will need regular supplies of paper. You may need to refer to the printer handbook to find out the correct method of refilling the paper trays. Dot matrix printers can sometimes be fiddly to refill and you will need to take care. Paper is produced in different weights and qualities. This is usually clearly labelled on the package and will tell you whether it is suitable to use in the printer you have. The weight of paper is measured in grams (gm). As a general guide, the all-purpose paper often used in photocopiers is 70–80gm.

When loading the paper for inkjets and lasers the paper should be the right way up – this is usually shown on the paper's packet by an arrow. When loading continuous paper in a dot matrix, you should check that the holes of the paper are located on the sprockets correctly.

When using acetates and other special paper, it is vital to check that you are using the correct type for the machine. Using the wrong one can jam the machine – or worse, can melt inside the printer, causing a great deal of damage.

You can print out sheets of labels on most printers, but you will need to check that you are using the correct ones for your printer.

Envelopes, too, can be used in most printers, but you will need to change the settings in the printer's menu to suit the size of envelope you are using.

This screen shot shows the printer settings for a Hewlett Packard Deskjet printer.

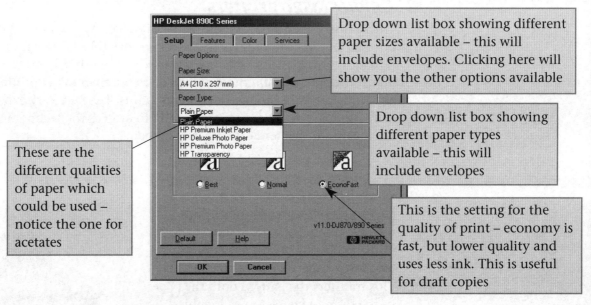

Figure 1.2 Printer settings

Try it out!

1 Look at the printer settings for your printer and list the different media you can use. (You may need to look in your printer manual or your Windows User Guide to access this dialogue box – or you could ask your tutor/instructor for advice.)

2 Decide which are the most common, for example A4 plain paper is probably what is used by most people most of the time, and collect examples of them. You should include examples of paper types (including acetates), envelopes and labels. Don't forget to write on them the size (and weight, if paper) of each one.

Changing the printer cartridges

It is very important to use the correct ink or toner in a printer. You will need to read the manual to find out the particular replacement you will need. The manual will also give you instructions on how to replace the cartridges – great care should be taken, especially when changing toner cartridges, which can be messy and dangerous.

When you have replaced the cartridge in a printer, it is often a good idea to print a test page to make sure that everything is working well. You will need to read your printer manual to find out how to do this. Quite often there will be an option in the printer menu to do this (as shown in the screen shot below) or a button on the front of the printer which will allow you to print a test page.

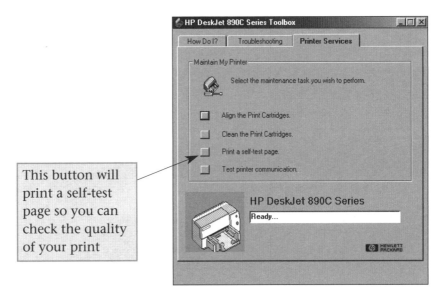

This button will print a self-test page so you can check the quality of your print

Figure 1.3 Printing a self-test page

To protect the environment, empty ink and toner cartridges should be disposed of with care. You may find that these empty cartridges can be sent back to organisations which will re-cycle them, often giving a donation to charity for every one returned. To help both the environment and a worthy cause, it's worth asking around to find the address of such an organisation. Some retail computer stores have envelopes available which can be used to return ink cartridges.

Try it out!

Use the printer manual for your printer to find out how to print a test page and print out a copy.

As with any piece of equipment, you have to treat printers with care. Even so, there are things that can sometimes go wrong, like the following:

- no page came out of the printer
- a blank page came out of the printer
- the text or graphics are in the wrong place
- print quality is poor
- something on the page is missing or incorrect

The solution could be anything from a paper jam to an empty ink cartridge. It is very important that you use the printer manual to find out what might be wrong and to either put it right according to the manual's instructions, or ask someone for assistance. You could do more damage if you try to 'have a go' yourself.

→ **Check your knowledge 3**

1 Label the various parts of the computer shown below.

2 A pixel is:
  a a small square on the screen
  b the size of a screen
  c the type of screen
  d a type of monitor

3 Many homes have inkjet printers because:
  a they are expensive to buy
  b they only print in black and white
  c they are noisy in operation
  d they are cheap to buy

4 Which of the following is the odd one out?
  When loading paper into a printer you must:
  a look to see if it's the right way up
  b use every sheet, even if it's creased
  c use the right paper for the printer
  d check in the manual if you're not sure how to load it

Modem

Your PC processes **digital** data, represented as either a 0 or a 1 (binary), by turning on or off a series of switches. Your telephone system is an **analogue** device which transmits signals in a continuous wave. A **modem** is a device which translates analogue signals into digital data and vice versa, and is called this because it **mo**dulates and **dem**odulates the signal so the telephone system and the computer can understand each other. You need a modem to connect to the Internet, usually via your telephone line, although newer technologies, such as cable, are now being used to connect to the Internet. The modem connected to your telephone can only transmit data up to a set rate. The speed that data is sent is measured in bits per second (bps) and the maximum rate of transfer over a standard phone line is 56 kilobits per second, represented as 56Kb.

Newer technologies, such as ISDN (Integrated Services Digital Network) and broadband, are much quicker than the traditional phone system, and are already used by businesses and large organisations.

Modems can be external or internal, but in either case they need to be connected to both your telephone line and your computer. To access the Internet you will need an ISP (Internet Service Provider) who will act as your 'gateway' to the Internet. Once connected to the Internet you can search the vast store of information (very useful for projects and homework), buy goods on-line (CDs and books are popular purchases), and send and receive e-mails.

A modem can also be used to send and receive faxes, either through your computer or from a fax machine attached to the phone line.

→ **Check your knowledge 4**

1 You would use a modem to:
   a word process a document
   b connect to a phone line
   c start up the computer
   d write an e-mail

Troubleshooting

Computers are very helpful tools when they are working, but as with all equipment, they sometimes develop problems or faults. Some of the most common problems which can happen when using your computer are:

- paper jams in the printer
- you forget to save your work and the computer crashes
- your floppy disk is damaged
- a computer cable has become loose
- a power cut occurs
- your mouse/keyboard has stopped responding.

It is very important that you can recognise when something has gone wrong. It isn't always possible for you to put it right and you might need to get someone to help you or to fix the problem. Using the manuals that come with your computer will provide many of the answers to these problems, but sometimes it is experience that can teach you how to cope when things go wrong.

Try it out!

In the Computer Faults & Errors Log below, record any problems that you have experienced when using your computer. You will need to record what went wrong and what you did to sort it out, or how you got help.

You will need to think about:
- whether it was a mistake you made
- whether it was an equipment fault
- whether the information you were given about what you had to do was clear or unclear
- how the incident affected your work
- where you went for advice
- what you did to put it right.

If you keep this log for a while and add to it whenever you meet a problem, you will have your own handy troubleshooting guide!

Computer Faults & Errors Log

Date	Error or fault	Effects (including how you put it right)

You will learn to

- Switch your computer on and close it down safely
- Identify types of software package
  - ☐ Describe the differences between applications software and systems software
- Identify an application software package which would be used to produce the following: letters and memos; slide shows; records of customers; financial accounts
- Use software
  - ☐ Load an application
  - ☐ Create a new document
  - ☐ Save a document
  - ☐ Close a document
  - ☐ Exit an application
  - ☐ Open an existing document
  - ☐ Edit a document and save as another file
- Set the software to automatically save
- Use a spellchecker
- Edit a document
- Use Help files and print information
- Use print preview
- Describe the purpose of a virus checker

Switching on and powering up the computer

Try it out!

Ensure that the computer is plugged in and power up your computer (switch it on!).

Hint:

You may need a password to log on to your network before you can reach this screen

When you switch on the computer it will look for the basic set of instructions in its ROM memory and begin to make some checks about the system. When it has completed its start-up checks and loaded the operating system you should see your **Windows desktop**, complete with **icons**, **mouse pointer** and **taskbar**. The items that appear on your screen will depend upon how your computer is set up, but it will look something like in Figure 2.1.

It is **very important** that you shut down a computer correctly – you don't just switch it off at the mains or use the on/off button. This could damage some of the data stored on the computer and could cause problems with some of your programs at a later date.

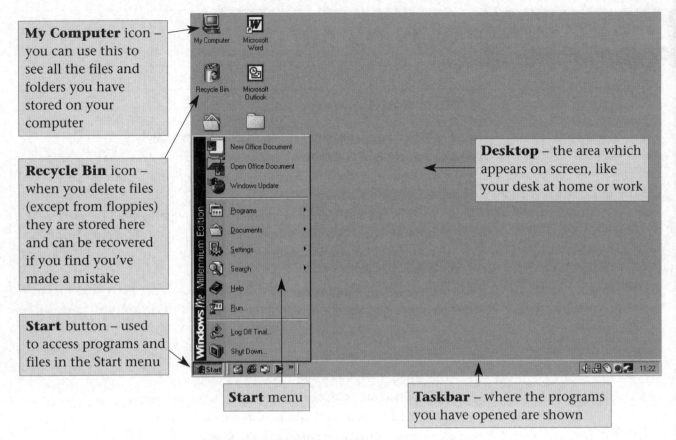

My Computer icon – you can use this to see all the files and folders you have stored on your computer

Recycle Bin icon – when you delete files (except from floppies) they are stored here and can be recovered if you find you've made a mistake

Start button – used to access programs and files in the Start menu

Desktop – the area which appears on screen, like your desk at home or work

Start menu

Taskbar – where the programs you have opened are shown

Figure 2.1 Screen items

Task 2.1 Shutting down your computer

1 Click on the Start button.
2 Select (click) **Shut Down** from the **Start** menu.

A **Shut Down Windows** dialogue box (a window asking for more information) will appear.

3 You will need to make sure that the correct option is chosen from the dialogue box. In this case, choose the **Shut Down** option.

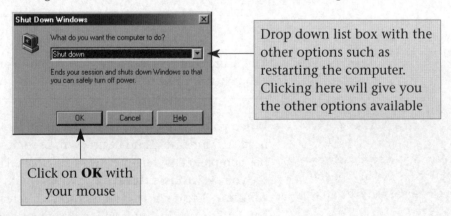

Drop down list box with the other options such as restarting the computer. Clicking here will give you the other options available

Click on **OK** with your mouse

Figure 2.2 Shut Down options

Don't switch off the power until you are sure that it is safe to do so. On some Windows operating systems, you may get a message telling you it is safe to turn off your computer.

Types of software

All computers need instructions which will tell them what to do. These instructions are computer codes called programs. They are referred to as **software**, and are usually stored on the hard disk until they are needed, and then they are transferred to the computer memory. Without software, the computer is just a collection of hardware bits and pieces, and would really be of little use to us in our day-to-day tasks. There are two types of software – **systems** software and **applications** software. Systems software includes the **operating** system and applications software are the programs which let us write a letter or work out our finances.

Operating system software

The operating software can be divided into two distinct parts. The first is a basic set of instructions the computer needs to start up and this is stored on the ROM (Read Only Memory) inside the computer. These instructions check the actual computer itself. The rest of the operating system is software which is loaded onto the computer and stored on the hard disk. This will let the computer manage and talk to all other parts of the computer system, such as peripherals and storage devices. It also allows you to access the other software on your machine, such as the word processing program to write a letter, as well as giving you ways to manage your files and information.

There are many operating systems such as UNIX, Linux, Mac OS, MS-DOS, but the most common operating system you will meet at work, school, college or home, is Microsoft's **Windows**. Windows is a **Graphical User Interface** (GUI) because it uses small pictures or graphics, called **icons**, **menus** and a pointing device, such as a **mouse**. This makes it much easier and friendlier to use, as you don't have to know or remember complicated commands.

Applications software

There is a vast array of applications software packages which will enable you to do many different things on your computer, but the most common are the following.

Word processing

A **word processing** program will let you enter text and then format it, change it and move it around. You can write documents such as letters, reports and memos, and even insert graphics and numbers. You can save the document to your hard disk or floppy to use again at a later date; in fact it is important to save your document regularly in case there are any problems with the computer or you need to leave it for a while.

Figure 2.3 A word processed document

You can also print out copies of the document to read or send to other people. This is probably the most commonly use program as it is something people will be using everyday to help them in their work. Microsoft Word is the word processing program you will be using to complete this module.

Information

There is a lot more to learn about using the Word application in the *Word Processing* book that is part of Heinemann's series for the Level 1 C & G Certificate for IT Users.

Spreadsheets

Percentage Meal types served per day							
	Day 1	Day 2	Day 3	Day 4	Day 5	Day 6	Day 7
Full Breakfast	68	82	75	75	79	59	62
H/made Cakes	12	10	10	13	11	23	24
Specials	20	8	15	12	10	18	14
Total	100	100	100	100	100	100	100

Figure 2.4 A spreadsheet

A **spreadsheet** is like a large sheet of paper divided into columns and rows to form a grid of **cells**. You can enter data into each cell and perform calculations using formulae. It is very useful to keep track of financial accounts or stock control and special buttons or menu items will allow you produce graphical representations of some of the data, using a bar chart or graph, for example. One of the benefits of a spreadsheet is that you can change some of the figures in a cell or cells and the spreadsheet will automatically re-calculate the new figures. Like the word processing program, a spreadsheet can be saved and changed at a later date and printed out when needed. Microsoft Excel is a spreadsheet program.

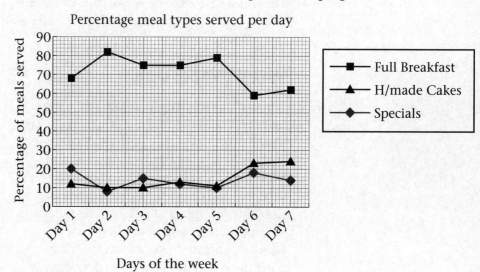

Figure 2.5 A graph

Database

A **database** is like a very complex filing system. It allows you to store data in an organised way so that you can find, search for and sort data very quickly in many different ways. A database could be used to keep a record of customers, and you would be able to search and sort the data to give you just the surnames of customers beginning with M, for example. This could take up a lot of time if it was all on paper, and a great deal of room to store, too. Databases can be saved and printed in the same way as other programs. Microsoft Access is a database program.

Ms Mariah Melling	106 Chestnut Street	D	N	Y
Mrs Patricia Philips	12 Elm Drive	N	Y	N
Ms Danni Maitland	14 Acacia Avenue	N	Y	N
Ms Kerry Howarth	14 Sycamore Road	N	N	Y
Ms Charlotte Jarvis	145 Wood Lane	D	Y	N
Ms Kate Thomas	165 Lilac Avenue	D	N	Y
Miss Laura Booth	17 Yew Tree Grove	G	Y	N
Mrs Michelle Collins	178 Wood Lane	G	Y	N
Ms Gwyneth Jowett	2 Lime Tree Avenue	G	N	N
Miss Claire Richards	21 Ash Boulevard	G	Y	Y
Mrs Danielle Brown	23 Beech Close	D	N	N
Mrs Alicia Simms	24 Fir Lane	N	Y	Y
Mrs Aretha McDowell	3 Elm Drive	D	N	Y
Mrs Maddy Palmer	32 Fir Lane	G	N	Y
Miss Jennifer Morgan	33 Apple Crescent	D	Y	N
Mrs Monica Haswell	4 Cherry Tree Lane	N	Y	Y
Mrs Joan Fernley	40 Acacia Avenue	G	Y	N
Miss Kylie Bleasedale	45 Chestnut Street	G	Y	N
Miss Elizabeth Dodd	56 Oaktree Road	G	Y	Y
Miss Jane Marple	6 Elm Tree Drive	N	N	Y
Mrs Mary Speakman	63 Birch Drive	N	N	N
Ms Madonna Reece	87 Walnut Grove	G	Y	N

Figure 2.6 A database

Presentations

You can use **presentation** software to create, design and organise slide shows to use when giving a talk for example, to help illustrate the points you want to make. The slides can be printed onto acetates to use with an overhead projector (OHP) or, using the computer and a special projector, they can be shown on a screen. Copies of the slides can be printed out for the people who come to listen to the presentation so that they can take them away for reference. Presentations can be saved for use later, or to make changes (editing). Microsoft PowerPoint is a presentation program.

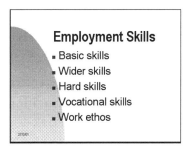

Figure 2.7 A presentation document

Desktop publishing

You can use **desktop publishing** (DTP) programs to create documents for publishing, such as posters, flyers, newsletters, etc. You can import, enter and manipulate text and graphics in a DTP program until you have a design which pleases you. Many word processing programs will also have some DTP features, but a 'top of the range' DTP package will produce copy ready for final printing. As with all the programs mentioned, you can save, edit and print out the results of your work. Microsoft Publisher is a DTP program.

Figure 2.8 A document produced by DTP

Information

There is much more to learn about spreadsheets, databases, desktop publishing and presentations in the *Spreadsheets*, *Databases*, *Presentation Graphics* and *Desktop Publishing* titles that are part of Heinemann's series for the Level 1 C & G Certificate for IT Users.

→ Check your knowledge 1

1 Operating system software is used to:
  a   produce a letter
  b   control the hardware and run programs
  c   design a newsletter or poster
  d   scan a document

2 Which of these would you do to shut down a computer?
  a   switch it off at the mains
  b   use the start button and menu
  c   switch it off at the power button
  d   unplug the computer

3 Match the following application software to the document it may be used to produce:
  a   word processor   i   newsletter
  b   spreadsheet   ii   memo
  c   DTP   iii financial account
  d   presentation   iv   record of clients
  e   database   v   slide show

4 Which of the following is not software?
  a   spreadsheet
  b   database
  c   mouse
  d   Microsoft Windows

5 Find out what operating system your computer uses.

Hint:

If you watch the screen closely when you start up your computer, it will tell you what operating system is installed. It could be Microsoft Windows 95, 98 or ME (Millennium Edition).

Try it out!

Find out what software applications are on your machine.

Before you begin, some mouse terms may be helpful:

- **Click**   Press and release the mouse button
- **Double click**   Click the mouse button twice, quite quickly.
- **Drag and drop**   If you want to move an object on the screen, select it with the mouse and click and hold the left mouse button. Keeping the mouse button pressed, move the object to another part of the desktop. Release the mouse button when the object is in the right place.
- **Hover**   Hold the mouse pointer over an object for a second or two and you may find a ToolTip or another menu will pop up. This will give you either information or suggestions. Try hovering your mouse pointer over the Start button.

First, however, you will need to switch on your computer to display your desktop.

1 Click on the **Start** button and move your mouse pointer up until it reaches **Programs**.

2 Hover your mouse pointer there, another menu will appear and you will be able to see the programs installed on your computer.

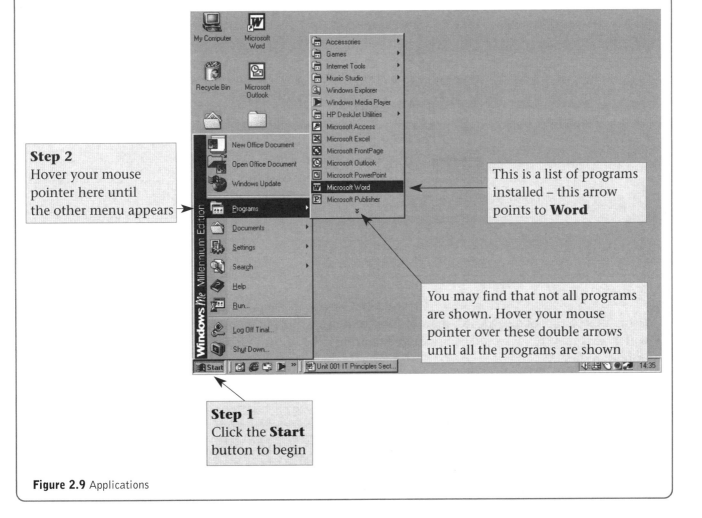

Step 2
Hover your mouse pointer here until the other menu appears →

This is a list of programs installed – this arrow points to **Word**

You may find that not all programs are shown. Hover your mouse pointer over these double arrows until all the programs are shown

Step 1
Click the **Start** button to begin

Figure 2.9 Applications

Using software

In this section you are going to start using a software application – Microsoft Word. Before you do, however, it would be helpful to get to know a little about your keyboard.

Some of the keys you will find yourself using often are:

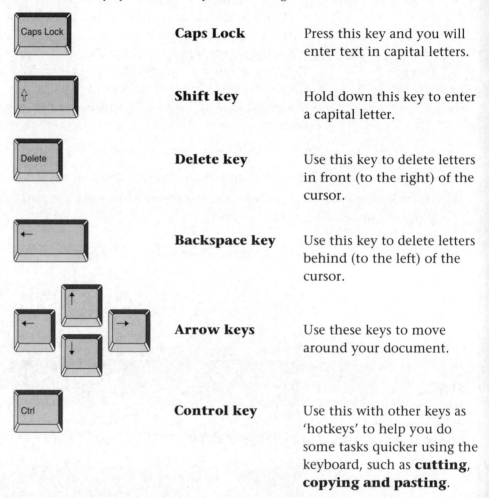

Caps Lock	**Caps Lock**	Press this key and you will enter text in capital letters.
Shift	**Shift key**	Hold down this key to enter a capital letter.
Delete	**Delete key**	Use this key to delete letters in front (to the right) of the cursor.
Backspace	**Backspace key**	Use this key to delete letters behind (to the left) of the cursor.
Arrows	**Arrow keys**	Use these keys to move around your document.
Ctrl	**Control key**	Use this with other keys as 'hotkeys' to help you do some tasks quicker using the keyboard, such as **cutting**, **copying and pasting**.

Try it out!

Using this picture of a keyboard, draw arrows to the keys already mentioned and write by the side which keys they are. It would be useful to add other notes to this picture as you come across other important keys.

A keyboard

1   Load up **Word** by clicking on the **Microsoft Word** item in the menu.

Information

If you have a shortcut icon to Word on your desktop, you can load

Word by double clicking on the 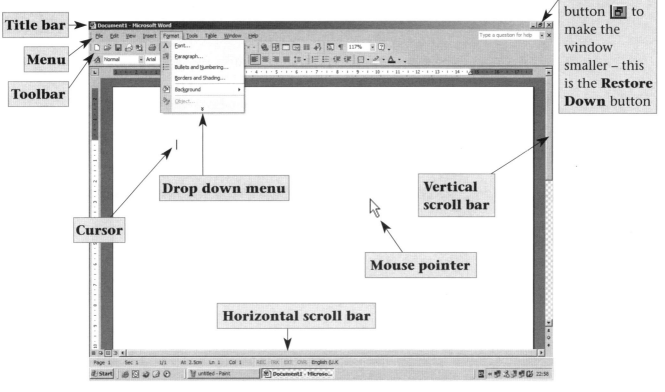 Word icon.

A **shortcut icon** is simply a quick way to start a program that you use often.

Hint:

When first open, Word always defaults to a blank document.

Your opening screen should look something like this:

Click this button to make the window smaller – this is the **Restore Down** button

Title bar

Menu

Toolbar

Cursor

Drop down menu

Vertical scroll bar

Mouse pointer

Horizontal scroll bar

Figure 2.10 An opening screen

Parts of the document window

- **Title bar**   This shows the name of the document (Document 9, in this case) and the program being used (Microsoft Word).

- **Menu bar**   This shows the menu names. Any of these menu items can be selected using the mouse or keyboard. A drop down menu will appear which will give you more options to choose from. You may need to hold your mouse pointer over the double arrows at the bottom of the drop down menu until all items are displayed as only the most recently used items are shown when the menu first drops down.

- **Toolbar**   There are different toolbars for different purposes. The **Standard toolbar** is where many of the most used functions are located such as **Print** and **Save**. These are buttons you can click on to choose the function shown by the picture.

- **Cursor**   This flashing bar shows where your text will be placed when you type into the document.

- **Scroll bars**   You can use these to move your view of the document up or down and side to side. This will let you see text that isn't showing in the window.

- **Mouse pointer**   This will move as you move the mouse and let you select items in the window. There are many designs for mouse pointers – this is the default (set up when first installed).

Task 2.3   Entering text

Using the keyboard, type in these words: 'The quick brown fox jumps over the lazy dog'. This is called **entering** text.

When you have done that, your document should look like this:

The quick brown fox jumps over the lazy dog

Figure 2.11 Entering text

Information

Hold down the **Shift** key before you type and you will enter a capital letter. If you want all capital letters, for a heading perhaps, press the **Caps Lock** key. (Remember to press it again when you want to go back to lower case!)

To enter a space between words, press the space bar on the keyboard. This is usually the long bar below the letter keys and often won't have anything shown on it to indicate what it does.

Try it out!

This involves taking a screen capture of your desktop.

You will now use a special function key (**Print Scrn**) and a 'hotkey' combination (**Ctrl + V**). You will also learn how to do a screen capture (sometimes called a screen shot, screen dump or screen grab). This will be very useful to you when you need to collect evidence as you complete the modules of this course.

1 Start up your computer until you have the desktop screen displayed. Press the '**Print Scrn**' button  on your keyboard (usually found in a little group of three keys to the right of your keyboard).

2 Open your word processing program and hold down the **Ctrl** key [Ctrl] (usually on the far left at the bottom of your keyboard). At the same time press the '**V**' key [V] on your keyboard (these are the 'hotkeys' to 'paste' into your document).

A picture of your desktop should have appeared in your word processing document.

Your document should look something like Figure 2.12.

Figure 2.12 Desktop

Print Scrn captures the image of the whole desktop. If you want to capture an image of the active window – the one which is being used, use the **Alt** [Alt] + **Print Scrn** keys instead.

Now you have used these hotkeys to take a screen capture of your desktop, remember to mark these keys on your keyboard picture (page 24).

Task 2.4 | Saving your work

It is always important to save your work regularly and often. You should get into the habit of doing this right from the moment you start to use a computer – it can save you a lot of frustration and tears at a later date!

Method

1   Click on the **Save** button 🖫 on the toolbar. The **Save As** dialogue box will appear.

2   Using the mouse, select **Floppy (A:)** from the drop down list box. (Make sure you have a floppy disk in the disk drive before you do this!)

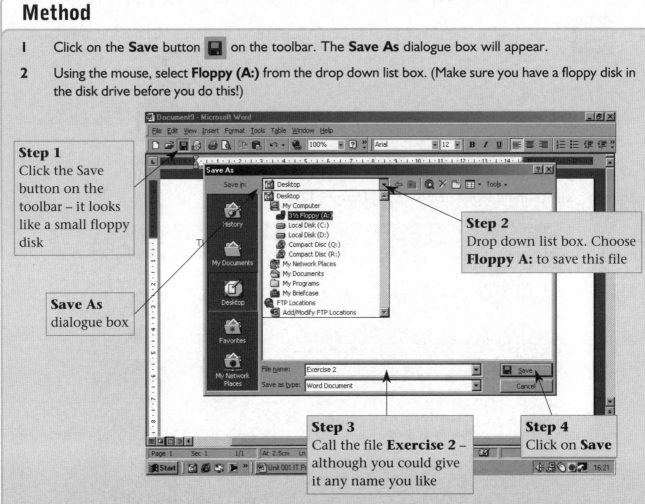

Step 1
Click the Save button on the toolbar – it looks like a small floppy disk

Save As
dialogue box

Step 2
Drop down list box. Choose **Floppy A:** to save this file

Step 3
Call the file **Exercise 2** – although you could give it any name you like

Step 4
Click on **Save**

Figure 2.13 How to save your work

3   Click in the **File name** box and type in **Exercise 2**. You could save it with any name you like, but for this exercise it is easier to save it as Exercise 2.

4   Click on the **Save** button.

Information

The screen shots in this book have been created using Windows ME (Millennium Edition) Operating system and Microsoft Office 2000. If you are using Windows 95 or 98 and Microsoft Office 97, you may find your **Save As** dialogue box looks slightly different. The steps for saving your files (and for all the following activities) are the same.

If you are using Windows 95 or 98 and Office 97, your **Save As** box might look like this:

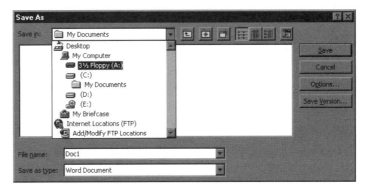

Figure 2.14 Save As dialogue box

Task 2.5 — Closing your application

Method

1 Click on the **File** button.
2 Select **Close** from the drop down menu, your document will close and you will be left with a blank window.
3 Click on the **File** button again, but this time select **Exit** from the drop down menu. Your application should now close and return you to your desktop.

Step 1
Click on the **File** button to drop down the menu

Step 2
Select **Close** from the menu and click on it

Step 3
To exit the program, click on the **File** menu again, and select **Exit** and click on it. This will close the application for you

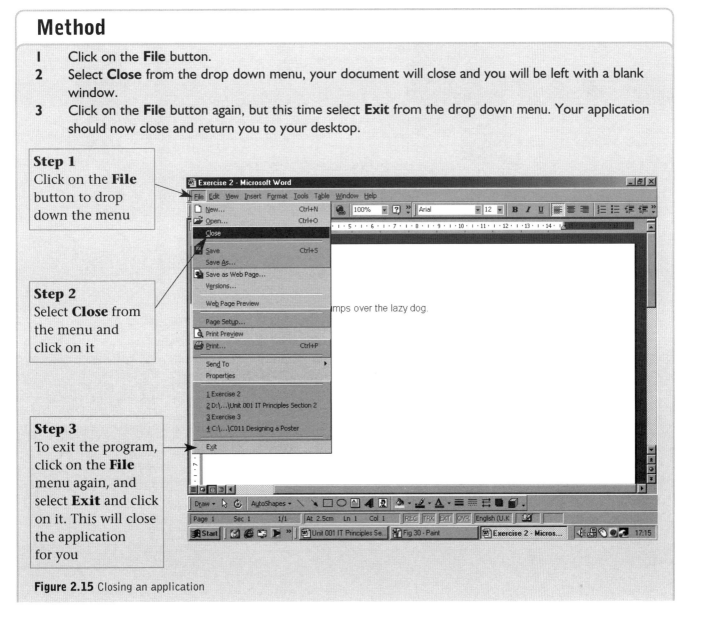

Figure 2.15 Closing an application

Method

Load your Word application.
1   Click on the **Open** button 📂 on the toolbar to access the **Open** dialogue box.
2   Using the drop down list box, select Floppy disk drive A: and click on it. (Make sure you have your floppy disk in the disk drive!)

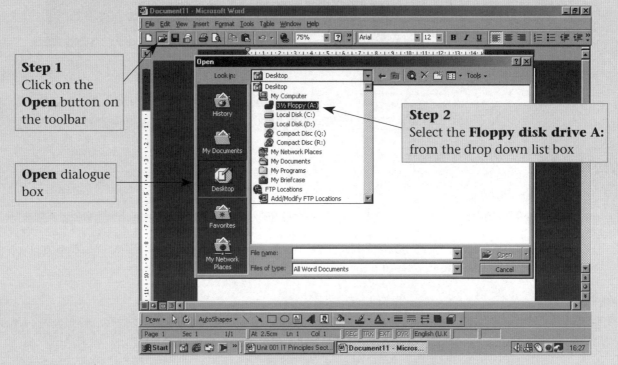

Step 1
Click on the **Open** button on the toolbar

Open dialogue box

Step 2
Select the **Floppy disk drive A:** from the drop down list box

Figure 2.16 Opening a document

Another **Open** dialogue box will appear which lists all the Word files you have saved to your floppy disk.
3   Select Exercise 2 with your mouse.
4   Click on the **Open** button.

Step 3
Click on the file you want – Exercise 2 in this case

Step 4
Click on the **Open** button to open your file

Figure 2.17 Opening a file

With Task 2.6 open in your Word program, you are going to add the word 'sometimes' to the end of the sentence.

Method

I	Move your mouse until the cursor is at the end of the word 'dog' and click the left button. This should place the cursor exactly where you want it to be – although you will need to put in a space using the space bar.
2	Type in the word 'sometimes'.

It's very useful to be able to save a file with another name. Perhaps you still want the original file, or maybe you are using the file to make a few different changes to see how it reads. Whatever the reason, you will need to **Save As** your document.

> Place your cursor at the end of the word 'dog', enter a space and the word 'sometimes'.

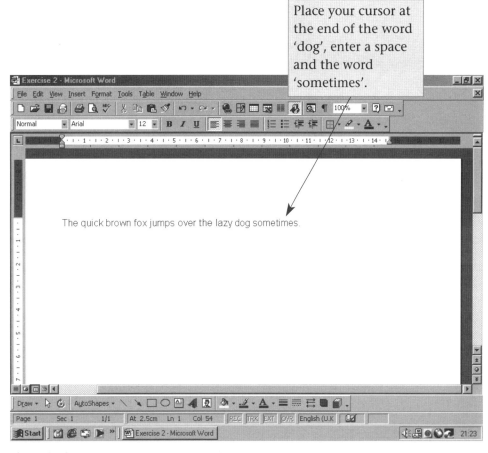

The quick brown fox jumps over the lazy dog sometimes.

Figure 2.18 Editing text

Task 2.8 | Saving with a new filename

To **Save** the changes to Exercise 2 with a new filename – in this case Exercise 3.

Method

I   Click on the File button on the menu bar and select the Save As option. This will open the Save As dialogue box.

If you were to just choose the **Save** button on the toolbar or the **Save** item in the menu the file would be saved as Exercise 2 **with the changes you have made**. You would have lost your old file Exercise 2. You can imagine how annoying that would be if you had wanted to keep the old file as well as the new file, especially if you had made a lot of changes along the way!

2   Select Floppy disk drive A: from the drop down list box.

3   Click in the **File name** box and type in the new filename – in this case Exercise 3.

4   Click on the **Save** button.

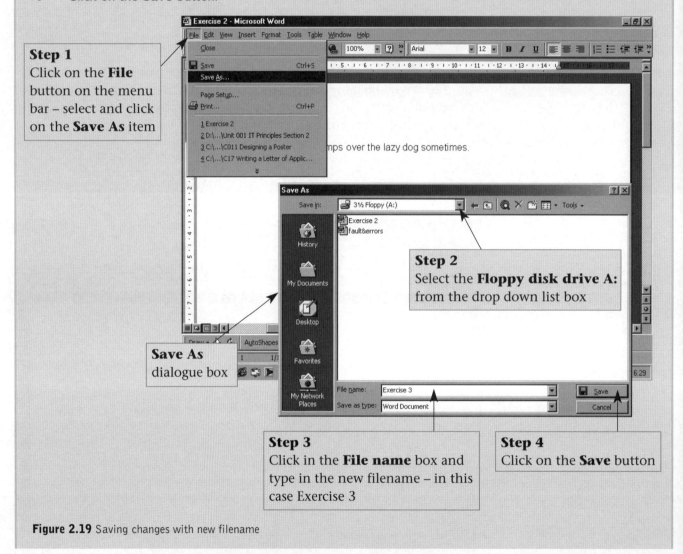

Step 1
Click on the **File** button on the menu bar – select and click on the **Save As** item

Step 2
Select the **Floppy disk drive A:** from the drop down list box

Save As dialogue box

Step 3
Click in the **File name** box and type in the new filename – in this case Exercise 3

Step 4
Click on the **Save** button

Figure 2.19 Saving changes with new filename

Auto saving

Remembering to save your work regularly is important, but sometimes it is easy to forget. Perhaps something distracts you, or the computer crashes. It can be very frustrating when that happens as you could lose hours of hard work. Many programs have an automatic save facility, and this can be helpful if the unthinkable happens.

Method

1   Select **Options** from the drop down **Tools** menu on the menu bar. The **Options** dialogue box will appear.
2   Click on the **Save** tab.
3   Click in the **Save AutoRecover info every:** to check the box. This selects the auto save option.
4   Select how often you want to auto save your file using the up and down arrows at the side of the **minutes** box.
5   Click on the **OK** button to accept the changes you have made.

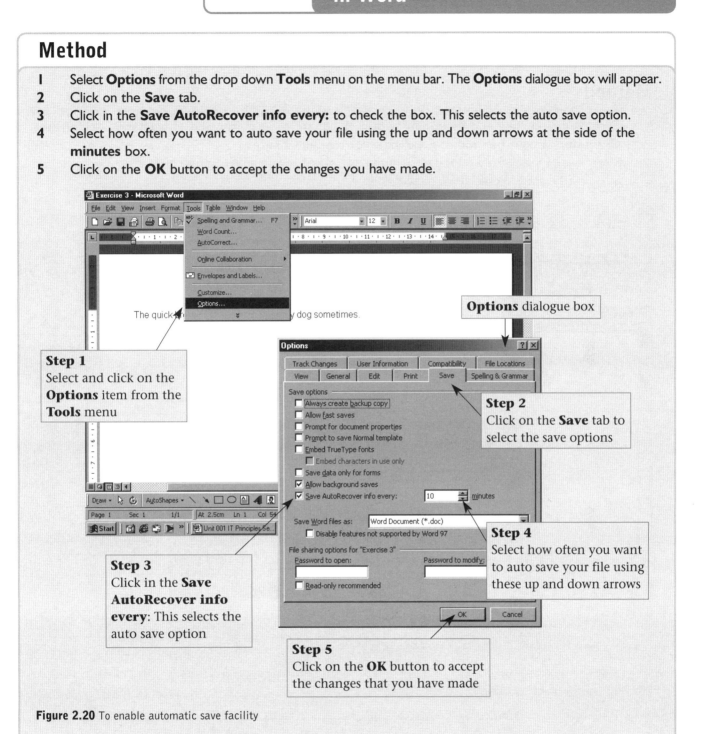

Figure 2.20 To enable automatic save facility

Spellchecking

A **spellchecker** can be a very handy option, especially if you want to produce a document without any spelling errors. One word of caution, however – a spellchecker can only find words which are spelt incorrectly by checking in its own dictionary. It can't tell the difference between there and their, as these would be spelt correctly, even if you used the wrong one in the wrong place! If you know you make mistakes like this, be careful whenever you type those tricky words.

Task 2.10 | Using a spellchecker

Method

1   Click on the **Spelling and Grammar** button 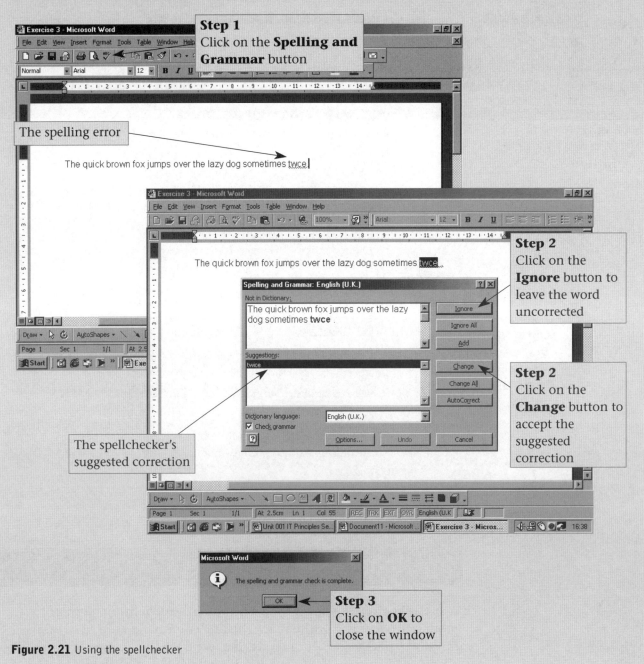 on the toolbar. This should open the **Spelling and Grammar** dialogue box with the spelling error highlighted in red.

2   Select one of the buttons on the right of the dialogue box to either **Change** or **Ignore** the suggestion made by the spellchecker in the pane below.

When the spellchecker has finished, a screen prompt will appear:

3   Click on **OK** to close the window.

Step 1
Click on the **Spelling and Grammar** button

The spelling error

The quick brown fox jumps over the lazy dog sometimes twce.

The quick brown fox jumps over the lazy dog sometimes twce.

Step 2
Click on the **Ignore** button to leave the word uncorrected

Spelling and Grammar: English (U.K.)

Not in Dictionary:
The quick brown fox jumps over the lazy dog sometimes **twce** .

Ignore
Ignore All
Add

Suggestions:
twice

Change
Change All
AutoCorrect

Step 2
Click on the **Change** button to accept the suggested correction

Dictionary language: English (U.K.)
☑ Check grammar
?   Options...   Undo   Cancel

The spellchecker's suggested correction

Microsoft Word
(i) The spelling and grammar check is complete.
OK

Step 3
Click on **OK** to close the window

Figure 2.21 Using the spellchecker

Method

- Using your document, Exercise 3, type in the word 'twce' (instead of twice) at the end of the sentence.
- Spellcheck your document.
- Accept the change.
- Save your file.

Information

You may have noticed that when you typed in 'twce', a red wavy line appeared under the word. This is Word's way of letting you know that there may be a spelling error. It can be a very useful function, but you will still need to look at the word carefully before you change it.

Office 2000's spellchecker also has a **Grammar** checker. Any errors in grammar which the program thinks you may have made, much like spelling errors, will be shown by a green wavy line. Just like a spellchecker, you will need to look at each suggestion made by the checker to see if you want to change your own text.

Editing a document

Information

Before you can edit text, you will need to enter it! Some useful pointers that you need to know:

- When you enter text into a document, you don't need to press the

  Enter key [⏎] at the end of each line – the text will

  automatically go onto the next line. This is known as **word wrap**.
- To leave a line between paragraphs you press **Enter** twice.

Task 2.12 | Selecting text

Method

1   Click in front of the text you want to select and hold down the mouse button.
2   Drag the I-beam along the text.
3   Release the mouse button when the text is selected.
4   The selected text will be highlighted as shown below.

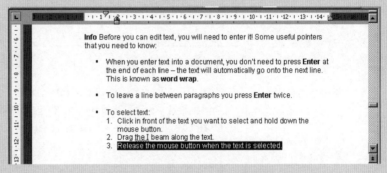

Figure 2.22 Selecting text

Task 2.13 | Inserting a letter or word into a document

Method

1   Click the mouse where you want the letter or word to go. This will put the I-beam in the right place.
2   Enter your letter or word.

Information

You can also delete a word or letter in the same way. Place your cursor in front of the letter or word you want to remove and press the **Delete** key. Alternatively, place your cursor behind the letter or word you want to remove and press the **Backspace** key (this is usually shown with a backwards facing arrow at the right-hand end of the top row of number keys).

→ Practise your skills 1

1 Load Word.
2 Open **Exercise 3**.
3 **Delete** the word 'twice'.
4 Insert the word 'very' in front of 'quick'.
5 Save your file as **Lazy dog**.
6 Close and exit Word.

→ Practise your skills 2

1 Load Word.
2 Open **Lazy Dog**.
3 Insert a line after 'sometimes'.
4 Enter the following text:

The lazy dog is called Rover, but it doesn't suit him at all. He likes to lie around the farmyard all day snoozing.

5 Save your file as **Rover**.
6 Close and exit Word.

Task 2.14	Copying and pasting text into a document

Sometimes it can be useful to be able to copy text from one document to another. This can save you time entering the text again. You may want to send the same information in letters you are writing to different people, for example.

Method

1 Select the text in your open document.
2 **Copy** the text using one of these three methods:

    (a) Click the **Copy** button 📋 on the toolbar.
    (b) Use the hotkeys **Ctrl + C**.
    (c) Select the **Copy** option from the **Edit** menu.

3 Open the document where you want to **Paste** the text.
4 Place the I-beam where you want the text to appear.
5 **Paste** the text using one of these three methods:

    (a) Click the **Paste** button 📋 on the toolbar.

    (b) Use the hotkeys **Ctrl + V**.

    (c) Select the **Paste** option from the **Edit** menu.

→ Practise your skills 3

1 Load Word.
2 Open your file **Rover**.
3 Copy the last paragraph.
4 Close your file.
5 Open your file **Exercise 2**.
6 Insert two lines after the word 'dog'.
7 Paste the paragraph at the end of the document.
8 Save the document as **Fox**.
9 Close and exit Word.

Information

You could **Cut** the text instead of copying by using one of these three methods:

1 Click the **Cut** button [✂] on the toolbar.

2 Use the hotkeys **Ctrl + Z**.

3 Select the **Cut** option from the **Edit** menu.

If you find that you've cut something by mistake, simply **Paste** it back into the document straight away and it should appear as if it never moved. You can also use the **Ctrl + Z** hotkey combination to **undo** your last bit of editing.

Help files

Sometimes it can be hard to recall everything that you need to remember when using any software program. Help is always at hand in the **Help files**, which you can access from the **Help** icon [?] on the toolbar or the **Help** button [Help] on the menu bar.

You can select different ways to find the help you need by clicking on the tabs. These are:

- **Contents** tab, which displays a list of help topics you can select from. This will often give you more detailed choices about the topic you have chosen.
- **Answer Wizard** tab, which allows you to type in a question, click on **Search**, and – Hey Presto! – a list of topics to choose from.
- **Index** tab, which is shown below.

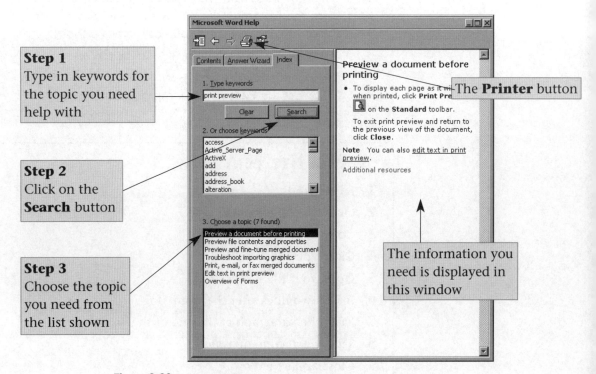

Figure 2.23 Using Help file

Try it out!

1 From the **Help** menu, search for help on 'print preview'. Select the appropriate topic and print out a copy.

2 Check the information in your printout with the details below about using the Print Preview button on your toolbar. Does it agree?

3 When you have compared the two pieces of information, load one of your documents and use the **Print Preview** button to see how it looks. Use the magnifying feature to zoom in on parts of the page.

Print preview and print

It can be very useful to see how your document will look before you print it out. It might be that you need to change some of the formatting, or perhaps put in some extra line spaces to make the document look more professional.

The **Print Preview** button 🔍 on the taskbar will allow you to preview your document. Clicking on this button will give you a screen like the one below:

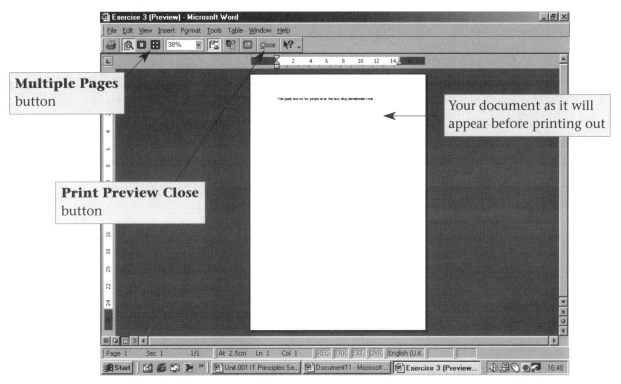

Figure 2.24 Using Print Preview to preview a document

The **Multiple Pages** button is useful when you have a longer document with several pages. It allows you to view more than one page at once.

When you pass your mouse pointer over the page it will change to a magnifying glass. You can click on any part of the page to zoom in closer to see more detail.

To close the window and return to your document window, click on the **Close** button.

When you've returned to the main document window, you may decide that you want to print out a copy.

To print out a copy of your document, click on the **File** menu and select the **Print** option.

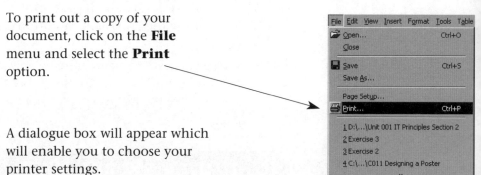

A dialogue box will appear which will enable you to choose your printer settings.

Remember to change the paper type, quality of print, orientation, and any other features you need before you click on the **OK** button – it can save you printing out a high quality print, which can use more ink and time, when all you wanted was a draft copy to see how your document looks

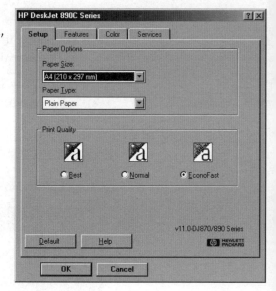

Figure 2.25 Choosing print options

If you know that you don't want to make any changes to your printer settings, you can use the **Printer** button ![printer icon] on the toolbar.

Error messages and screen prompts

As you complete these exercises you may have come across some error messages or screen prompts. Even if you haven't as yet, you are sure to meet both of them during your time spent at a computer. These messages and prompts can be helpful, like reminding us to save our work, or telling us that something isn't working properly. Some, however, can seem to be meaningless to the ordinary computer user, and then, perhaps, it's time to consult an expert.

Some of the messages and prompts you might meet could look like the examples which follow:

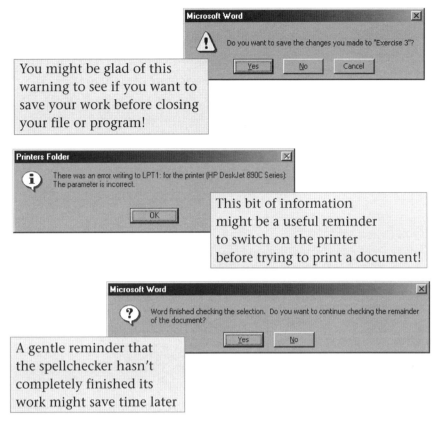

You might be glad of this warning to see if you want to save your work before closing your file or program!

This bit of information might be a useful reminder to switch on the printer before trying to print a document!

A gentle reminder that the spellchecker hasn't completely finished its work might save time later

Figure 2.26 Messages and prompts

Whenever a screen prompt appears, read it carefully and then decide what you want to do. If you want to accept the suggestion, you would click the **OK** button. If you don't want to accept the suggestion, click on **No**. If there's a third option – **Cancel** – this gives you a chance to go back to where you were and think again about what you want to do!

If, on the other hand, you get an error message, you can be sure the computer is trying to tell you something important. It often means that you have asked it to do something it isn't sure about or doesn't like. Read the message carefully and decide if it's something you can sort out (like turning on the printer because you had forgotten to do so!), then you can click the **OK** button. If it's something that you can't make head or tail of, it might be best to leave the message on the screen and seek help. That way the expert will know what the computer is trying to tell you.

Try it out!

It would be worth keeping a list of any unusual error messages or screen prompts for future use, especially if they aren't ones you've seen before which you can interpret easily. It would build into your own reference source. Don't forget that the **Help files** might also be able to sort out your problems.

1 Put these steps in the correct order to save a file:
   a click on the **Save** button on the toolbar
   b click on the **Save** button on the **Save As** dialogue box
   c choose where to save your file
   d give your file a name

2 To open a document saved on a floppy disk you would firstly:
   a click on the **Open** button on the toolbar
   b click on the **File** button on the menu bar
   c click on the **Open** button on the **Open** dialogue box
   d make sure the floppy is in the floppy disk drive

3 The **Save As** option is used to:
   a save your file with a different name
   b save your file with the original name
   c delete your file
   d make changes to your original file

4 Which of the following sentences would the spellchecker show as having a spelling error?
   a He could here the music from the speakers.
   b She was two tired to go out in the evening.
   c When you have finished you must switch of your computer.
   d We have our computer lessons on a Wednsday.

5 The **Print Preview** button will let you:
   a save your document
   b see your document before you print it
   c check that the printer is switched on
   d check your spelling

Virus checkers

A **virus** is a small piece of code deliberately buried inside a computer program to cause mischief. When the program is run, the virus starts running too. Some viruses are written as a joke to display a message on your screen or make your computer beep every now and then. Others can do a lot of damage to the data in your files and even erase all the information on your hard drive. There are thousands of different viruses and new ones are being invented all the time.

Viruses can spread, just like a cold, from computer to computer. They spread by infecting other disks or by attaching themselves to files you've downloaded from the Internet. If you save a file to a disk from a computer with a virus and then load the file into your own computer, the virus is loaded as well!

As quickly as a new virus is invented, so an 'antidote' to it is developed. The software which can find and clean out a virus is called **anti-virus** software. This software will check all your files to see if any viruses are lurking and will make sure that they are 'disinfected'. Anti-virus software can be used to scan (check) just one file or all the files on your hard drive or floppy; it will depend on how you set up the software. Anti-virus software is usually called a **utility** program.

It is important to update your anti-virus software regularly so that it can detect any of the newer viruses and eliminate them from your machine.

Some golden rules for preventing a virus attack

- Buy a good anti-virus utility – and make sure you use it often!
- Don't share disks. If it can't be avoided, make sure you run a virus check before opening the file.
- Take care when downloading files from the Internet. Run your virus checker – or set it to run automatically.
- Don't use your floppy disks in lots of different computers if you can avoid it – the more computers you use, the greater the chance of catching a virus.
- Use only commercial software – they will have been checked for viruses before being produced.
- Be careful about loading programs which are free or second hand, they could have a virus lurking quietly waiting to strike!

Try it out!

Find out if the computer you use has an anti-virus utility installed.

→ Practise your skills 4

1 Switch on your computer and load Word.
2 Open a new document and type the following sentence:
   'I must remember to save my work.'
3 Save the file to your floppy disk with the filename **practice 1**.
4 Close the file and exit Word.
5 Load Word again and open your file **practice 1**.
6 Add the word 'regularly' to the end of the sentence.
7 Save your file with the filename **practice 2**.
8 Close your file and exit Word.

→ Practise your skills 5

1 Load Word.
2 Open your file **practice 2** and check the spelling.
3 Insert two lines after the word 'regularly'.
4 Enter the following text:
If I forget to save my work and then something goes wrong, I could lose all the work I've done. I would feel very cross.
5 Save your file.
6 Preview your file and then print a copy.
7 Close your file and exit Word.

→ Practise your skills 6

1   Load Word.
2   Enter the heading:
    SAVING MY WORK
3   Insert a line after the heading and save your file as **practice 3**.
4   Open your file **practice 2**.
5   Copy all the text and close the file.
6   Paste the text under the heading.
7   Save your file.
8   Close and exit Word.
9   Close down your computer.

Section 3 | Management skills

You will learn to

- Identify measurements of data storage
- Identify data storage devices
  - ☐ Describe the importance of careful handling and data storage
  - ☐ Describe the importance of backing up data
- Describe a computer filing system
  - ☐ Describe a basic directory and folders structure
  - ☐ State the difference between directories and files
  - ☐ Create, delete and re-name files and subdirectories
  - ☐ Copy and move files between directories
  - ☐ Copy and move files to a floppy disk
  - ☐ Make backup copies of files to a disk
- Save data to a hard disk
- Search for named files
- Describe the importance of data protection, confidentiality and copyright
  - ☐ Identify ways to prevent the loss of data

Every time you use a computer to do your work, you will want to save and manage your files, just as you would do if they were all paper-based documents. Before finding out the skills to keep your files in order, it would be helpful to know about the different ways of storing and saving files.

Measurements of data storage

A computer processes **digital** data, represented as either a 0 or a 1, by turning on and off a series of switches. This is called **binary code**. A **bit** is the smallest unit of storage or memory and each character of information, such as the letter b, is made of eight **bits**. This is known as a **byte**.

So a character (a letter, number, symbol or space) would look something like this to the computer:

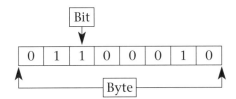

A **byte** is used to measure the space on a computer storage device.

As a byte is very small, storage measurements are usually represented as **kilobytes, megabytes** or **gigabytes**.

8 bits   = 1 byte
1000 bytes = 1 kilobyte (approximately), written as **Kb** or **K**
1000 Kb   = 1 megabyte (approximately), written as **Mb**
1000 Mb   = 1 gigabyte (approximately), written as **Gb**

Devices for storage of data

Keeping your data safe

If you want to keep your data safe you will need to make sure that it is stored in a **non-volatile** storage device (where the data isn't lost when the computer is switched off). There are several different ways to store data safely, and which one you use will depend on factors such as:

- Do you want to move the information from one machine to another?
- What size are the files? They may be too large for some storage devices like floppy disks.
- What storage devices are available on your machine?
- How quickly do you want to save the data?
- Will your data be safe on the storage device you have chosen?

These are some of the most common storage devices:

Hard disk

The **hard disk** is a magnetic plate or series of plates which hold data as magnetised spots on the disk surface and is usually located inside the computer case. The disk has a large amount of storage space (measured in megabytes or gigabytes) and the data on a hard disk can be read much quicker than from a floppy disk. Programs that you load onto the computer, such as your word processing program, are stored on the hard disk so they are available when you need them.

A hard disk

USB compact flash memory

Amazingly, this is a gadget, hardly bigger than your little finger, which can be plugged into your computer's USB (Universal Serial Bus) port to store many times more data and files than a pair of floppy disks. This device has several names, including pen drive, portable drive and memory stick. Using 'plug and play' technology, you don't have to load any new software onto your computer, simply plug the device into a spare USB port, and you can use it straightaway. It will be shown in **My Computer** as a **removable storage device** alongside your CD or DVD-ROM drive, with a drive letter

Removable
Disk (E:)

such as (E:) The USB portable storage devices can hold anything from 32MB of data to 256MB, and make transferring files and information from one computer to another very quick and easy.

home, for example. They will only hold a small amount of data, usually 1.44Mb, although that is much the same as an entire book full of information. Most floppy disks today are $3\frac{1}{2}''$, and fit into the $3\frac{1}{2}''$ floppy disk drive on your computer. They are cheap, light to carry and easy to use.

Although floppy disks come in a hard case, it is still important to take care of them.

Some golden rules for floppies

- Always store your disks carefully away from magnetic fields such as televisions or motors.
- Never touch the coated plastic disk inside the hard case.
- Label and file your disks carefully.
- Be careful how you write on the label – too much pressure with a ballpoint pen could damage the disk surface.
- Don't leave your disks in the sunlight or near radiators.
- Write-protect your disk to keep your data safe.

Before you can use a new floppy disk, you may need to **Format** it. Most disks are already formatted to use straight away, but if not, you will need to format it before you can save your work. Formatting prepares your disk so that the computer can store information on it.

Task 3.1   Formatting a floppy disk

Method

1 Open **My Computer**.
2 Use right-hand mouse to click on the A: drive icon.
3 Move down the menu which appears and select the **Format** option.
4 In the **Format** dialogue box which appears, select the disk capacity.
5 Select the **Full** option.
6 Click on **Start**.

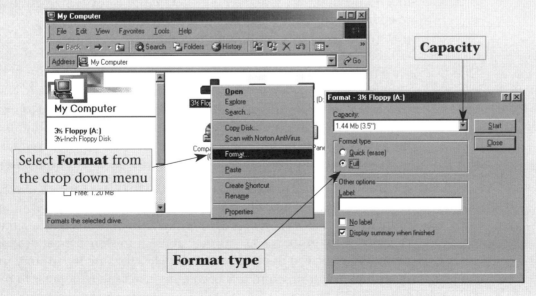

Figure 3.1 Formatting a floppy disk

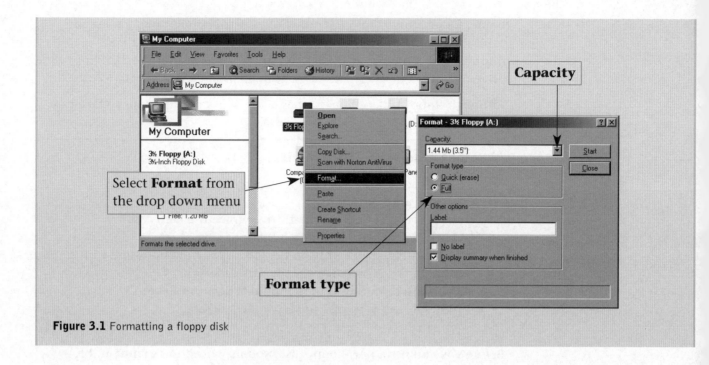

Select **Format** from the drop down menu

Capacity

Format type

Figure 3.1 Formatting a floppy disk

Information

Most floppy disks will be high density – 1.44Mb. Some older disks may be 720Kb and are called double density. You can tell a high density disk from the two holes at the bottom.

Optical devices

Optical storage devices are ideal for holding large amounts of data that doesn't need updating, and for storing large programs. CD-ROMs are often filled with clip art, photographs, video clips and large amounts of text. This is called **multi-media**.

A **CD-ROM** (Compact Disc Read Only Memory) looks like the compact disc used for music and works in much the same way. A high-energy laser beam is used to etch patterns onto a special surface and the patterns are read by a low intensity beam in the CD-ROM drive. Once the patterns have been etched onto the surface of the CD they can't be changed, although they can be read many times by the computer.

A compact disc

CDs can store large amounts of data (over 500 times the data on a floppy), and can be used to store whole encyclopaedias, including sound files and images, as well as the software for programs to use on your computer. The computer can read the data on a CD much quicker than from a floppy.

A **CD-R** (Compact Disc-Recordable) is a CD that you can use to record your data. You will need a CD-R drive to do this, but a CD-R drive can read ordinary CD-ROMs as well as CD-R disks. CD-R disks have the same storage capacity as an ordinary CD, so you can use it to store a great deal of information instead of using lots of floppies. Because it can store such large quantities of information, it is becoming increasingly popular to record music to CD-Rs and use in a CD player away from the computer.

A **CD-RW** (Compact Disc-Rewritable) is used in the same way as a blank music tape. It can be recorded on again and again. It has all the advantages of a CD-R, but you can change the data stored on it, much like a floppy. You will need a CD-RW drive to do this, although a CD-RW drive will also read CD-R disks and CD-ROMs. CD-RW disks are slightly more expensive than CD-R disks.

A **DVD** (Digital Video/Versatile Disc) is another optical device very similar to a CD-ROM, although a shorter wavelength laser is used to read the patterns on the surface. DVDs can store huge amounts of data – roughly equivalent to 13 CDs – and are often used to store the massive quantity of data for a whole movie. DVDs can be used in computers with a DVD drive or in special DVD players which can be linked to your television. Recordable DVDs and DVD drives are also available, but are quite expensive at the moment although they will probably be part of the home computer package in the not to distant future.

All optical storage devices should be treated with the same care you would give to your music CDs:

- Handle CDs by the edges, don't touch the recording surface.
- Keep away from heat sources and don't leave them lying in the sun.
- Always put them back into their protective wallet or case after use.
- Don't scratch the surface of the CD.

Other storage devices

Zip disk

A **zip disk** looks similar to a floppy disk and, like a floppy, it can be removed from one zip drive and used in the zip drive of another machine. It can store more data than a floppy, between 100–250Mb, which makes it useful for holding large files. Zip drives can be built into the computer (internal) or attached to the computer by special cables (external). The computer can read the data from a zip disk quicker than it can from a floppy disk.

Magnetic tape

Magnetic tape can be used to store large amounts of data, but is usually used for backups and archives (data stored away as a record). Many large organisations will use magnetic tape to backup (take a copy of) the data on the computer. If any problems arise with the data on the computer, the information can be restored to its original form from the backup tape. Tapes can be stored away from the computer, keeping them safe if anything goes wrong. Imagine what a fire might do to the information on a computer – a backup tape would be very welcome in those circumstances! Tape storage is slower than other storage devices as the data stored on it has to be read from the beginning, even if the bit of data needed is right at the end of the tape. Many companies will have their computers set to automatically back up the system overnight.

As with your floppies and CDs, care should be taken when storing your zip disks or magnetic tapes:

- Keep away from magnetic sources.
- Store away from extremes of heat.
- Always store them in their protective cases when not in use.
- Label them carefully.
- Don't touch the recording surface.

Backing up your data

If you remember that data is stored as a 0 or a 1 onto one of the storage devices, you'll realise how easy it would be for the data to be damaged, so it is important to keep your data safe. One way to do this is to make backup copies of your files so that if the worse happens and your files are lost or your disk gets damaged, you will have a copy of your data to use. You could use any of the storage devices to do this; it will depend on the equipment you have on your computer.

One thing you will need to remember is that you need to keep your backup copies safe too!

Information

A virus utility can also help to prevent loss of your precious data, but only if you update it regularly and use it often!

→ Check your knowledge 1

1 Volatile memory is:
   a   CD-RW
   b   Hard disk
   c   RAM
   d   DVD

2 Lasers are not used in:
   a   CD drives
   b   DVD drives
   c   floppy drives
   d   CD-R drives

3 You would store the programs you use often on a:
   a   magnetic tape drive
   b   floppy disk
   c   zip drive
   d   hard drive

4 A high density floppy disk stores:
   a   1.44 Gb of data
   b   1.44 Kb of data
   c   1.44 Mb of data
   d   1440 bytes of data

5 When storing your floppy disks you should:
   a   keep them in a warm place
   b   leave them on your desk
   c   use a disk box to keep them safe
   d   make sure they're near a magnetic field

6 You should back up your data to help prevent:
   a   losing all your work
   b   other people looking at your files
   c   copying your work
   d   cluttering up your hard drive

A computer filing system: My Computer

Behind the Windows desktop is a filing system that keeps all the computer's information in order. This includes your own information and the programs that run the computer. One way of describing it is to compare it to a filing cabinet. The cabinet is the directory, the drawers are the subdirectories, and inside the drawers are dividers known as folders which hold all the information required in files.

Just like any well-organised filing system, the folders are usually shown in alphabetical order. This makes it easy to find a folder called 'Practical Tasks' by scrolling through the folders list to find those beginning with 'p'.

The information is stored in a **directory** and **folder** structure, which looks like this:

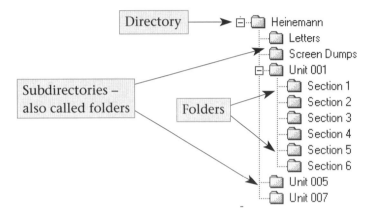

Figure 3.2 Storage of information

This is like a tree. It has a main trunk with branches, though only on one side in this case!

Inside the **directory** are subdirectories or **folders**, and inside each of the folders there would be files and possibly some more folders.

Task 3.2 | Viewing the files inside the folders

Method

I Double click on the **My Computer** icon on your Windows desktop.
You should find a screen much like this one shown in Figure 3.3.

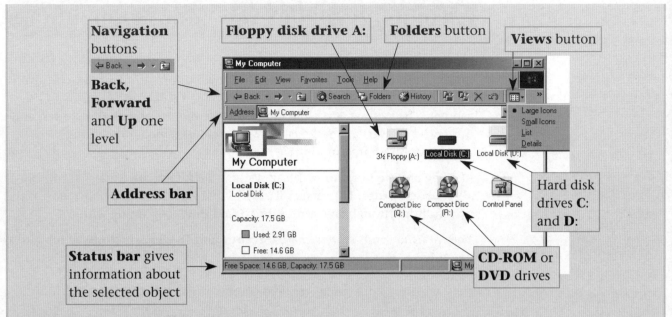

Figure 3.3 Computer filing/storage system

Don't worry if your screen looks a little different, as there are several ways of showing the information.

2   Click on the **Views** button on the taskbar and choose one of the options from the drop down menu. The view above shows the objects as **large icons**.

Your computer may not show the same number of hard disk drives – this computer has two, C: drive and D: drive, and also two compact disc drives, Q: and R:.

If you double click on the hard disk drive icon, this will open up to show the folders and files stored in the drive.

To see another view you will find useful as you manage your files, click on the **Folders** button on the taskbar.

This will show you all the directories, folders and drives on your computer in the left-hand pane, and make moving files around easier.

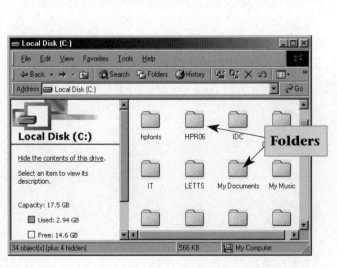

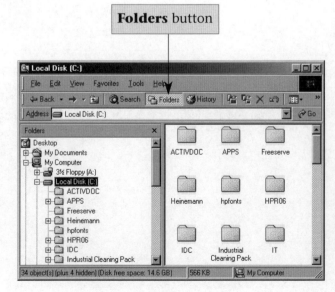

Figure 3.4 Folders and files

Inside the folders will be files and perhaps more folders. Files are shown in a different way to folders, so it is easy to tell the difference. Double click on a folder icon to show the contents inside.

This is an example of a **folder**.

This is an example of a **file**. When you save your work to a floppy disk or a hard drive, it becomes a file. The icon above the filename tells you what type of file it is. This is a Word file.

Types of file

There are many different types of file, so it may be helpful to be able to recognise some of the most common ones.

When you save a file you give it a filename which tells you what the file may be about (it's worth trying to use filenames that indicate the contents, otherwise you can end up opening lots of files to find the one you want). The computer also adds a bit of information in the form of three letters, called the file **extension**, which tells the computer which software application was used to create the file, or what type of file it is.

Your file **Rover** was created using Word. The computer will add a full stop after **Rover**, and add the letters **doc**. To the computer, your filename is **Rover.doc**. The **doc** extension tells the computer that it is a Word file.

Some other common extensions are:

.xls   Microsoft Excel
.mdb   Microsoft Access
.ppt   Microsoft PowerPoint
.bmp   Paint
.rtf   Rich Text Format (most word processing programs can read these files)
.txt   Notepad
.htm   HTML files used on the World Wide Web

Some of the files needed by the computer to operate the software and systems also have extensions. These are files which you shouldn't need to do anything with at all. In fact, if you changed or deleted these files, your computer might stop working.

Some of these files will have extensions such as .exe, .com, .dll, .bat, .ini.

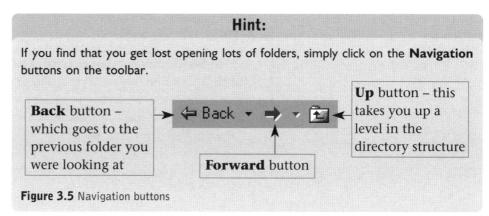

Figure 3.5 Navigation buttons

Information

The screen shots in this book were taken using Windows ME (Millennium Edition) Operating system. If you are using Windows 98 you will need to open **Windows Explorer** instead of **My Computer**, which can be found in your Programs menu.

Task 3.3 — Accessing Explorer

Method

1   Click on **Start**.
2   Move up the menu to **Programs**.
3   Select **Explorer** from the next menu.

Your window should look similar to this:

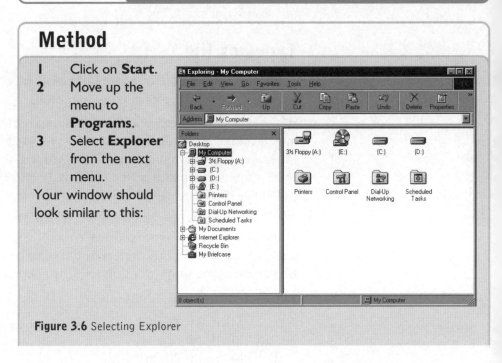

Figure 3.6 Selecting Explorer

The methods in the following tasks will work for both Windows ME and 98, unless indicated otherwise.

You can create new folders to keep your work in order. Perhaps you would want to keep all your business letters in one folder and all your personal letters in another. You can nest folders inside other folders, or add new folders to the main directory – it will all depend on how you want to organise your data.

Task 3.4 — Creating a new folder in your C: directory

Method

1   Open **My Computer** and click on the C: drive icon.
2   Click on the **File** button on the toolbar.
3   When the menu drops down, move the pointer down to the **New** item, and a new menu will appear.
4   Select **Folder** from the submenu.
5   Type in the name of the new folder and press **Enter** on the keyboard.

Information

You may need to scroll down the right-hand pane of the window to find the new folder – it may be at the end of all the files.

There are often other ways of getting things done on a computer. You may find other ways which suit you better.

This is another way of creating a folder:

Method

1	Click in the right-hand pane with your **right mouse button**.
2	Move your pointer down the menu which appears, to **New**.
3	Select **Folder** from the submenu.

You may find this way quicker, especially as you get used to using your right mouse button.

To create a subfolder (subdirectory) within your newly created folder (directory):

Method

1	Click on your new folder.
2	Use one of the methods above to create your new subfolder.

Try it out!

Create two new folders (directories) and name them **Section 2** and **Section 3**.

Task 3.5   Copying a file or folder

Method 1

1	Select the file/folder you want to copy.
2	Select **Copy** from the **Edit** menu on the toolbar.
3	Select the directory, drive or folder where you want to copy the file/folder.
4	Select **Paste** from the **Edit** menu on the toolbar.

Method 2

1	Select the file/folder you want to copy with the right mouse button.
2	Select **Copy** from the menu which appears.
3	Select where you want to copy the file/folder with the right mouse button.
4	Select **Paste** from the **Edit** menu which appears.

Method 3

I	Select the file/folder.
2	Hold down the right mouse button and drag the file/folder to where you want it to be copied.
3	Release the mouse button.
4	Select **Copy here** from the menu which appears.

Method 4

I	Select the file/folder.
2	Use the hotkey combination **Ctrl + C** to copy it.
3	Select where you want to copy the file/folder.
4	Use the hotkey combination **Ctrl + V** to paste it.

Try it out!

For this you will need your floppy disk with two of the files you saved in Section 2. They were called **Exercise 2** and **Exercise 3**.

- Copy the file **Exercise 2** to your new folder **Section 2**.

If you open your folder Section 2, you should see a copy of your file there.

Information

If you are using a computer which is networked, you may need to find out which area of the network you can create your new folders in and move your files around.

See Section 5 for more information about networks and the rights to create new folders on a network drive.

Task 3.6   Moving a file or folder

Moving files or folders is done in much the same way as copying, but choosing slightly different options:

Method 1

I	Select the file/folder you want to copy.
2	Select **Cut** from the **Edit** menu on the toolbar.
3	Select the directory, drive or folder where you want to put the file/folder.
4	Select **Paste** from the **Edit** menu on the toolbar.

Method 2

I   Select the file/folder you want to copy with the right mouse button.
2   Select **Cut** from the menu which appears.
3   Select where you want to put the file/folder with the right mouse button.
4   Select **Paste** from the **Edit** menu which appears.

Method 3

I   Select the file/folder.
2   Hold down the left mouse button and drag the file/folder to where you want to move it.
3   Release the mouse button.

Method 4

I   Select the file/folder.
2   Use the hotkey combination **Ctrl + X** to cut it.
3   Select where you want to put the file/folder.
4   Use the hotkey combination **Ctrl + V** to paste it.

Try it out!

For this you will need your floppy disk with two of the files you saved in Section 2. They were called **Exercise 2** and **Exercise 3**.

1   Copy the file **Exercise 2** to your folder **Section 3**.
2   Move the file **Exercise 3** to your new folder **Section 2**.

If you open your folder Section 2, you should see both your files there.

Check your floppy disk, by clicking on the floppy disk icon in the left-hand pane, to make sure that the file **Exercise 3** has gone.

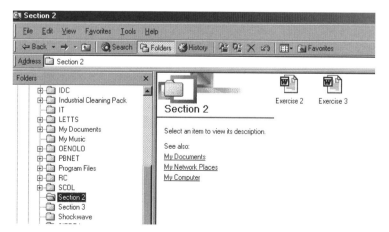

Figure 3.7 Copying and moving files to folders

Task 3.7　Renaming files/folders

Method

1　Right click on the file/folder.
2　Select **Rename** from the menu.
3　Type in the new name.

Try it out!

1　Open the folder **Section 3**.
2　Rename the file in there **Exercise 4**.
3　Copy the file to the folder **Section 2**.
4　Open your folder **Section 2** to check the files.

You should have all three files in your Section 2 folder.

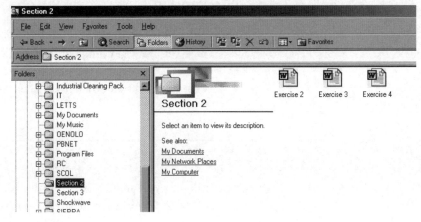

Figure 3.8 Renaming a file

Task 3.8　Copying and moving files and folders to a floppy disk

The process for copying and moving files and folders to a floppy disk is exactly the same as for copying and moving files and folders to a hard drive or between folders and directories.

Try it out!

1　Move the file **Exercise 4** from the folder **Section 3** to your floppy disk.
2　Copy the file **Exercise 3** from the folder **Section 2** to the floppy disk.

You should have all three files on your floppy disk. This has given you a backup copy of your files.

If you have completed these tasks successfully, you will have an empty folder **Section 3**. If you find that you have files or folders you no longer need, you can **Delete** them by sending them to the **Recycle Bin**.

The Recycle Bin is an area of your hard drive where files and folders which you have deleted are stored. This is a safety net for you so that you can restore the file if you've deleted it in error. It's good practice to leave files in your Recycle Bin for a few weeks to see if you need them or not before **emptying** your bin. Files in your Recycle Bin will still take up space on your hard drive, so it's good housekeeping to empty it from time to time.

Task 3.9 — Deleting files/folders

Method

1 Select the file/folder.
2 Press the **Delete** key on your keyboard.
3 If you are sure you want to delete the file/folder, click the **Yes** button on the prompt box which has appeared.

Try it out!

Delete the folder **Section 3**.

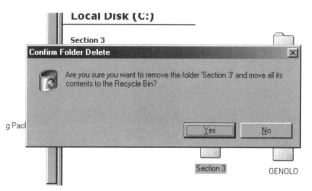

Figure 3.9 Deleting a folder

Your folder should now be in the Recycle Bin – click on the Recycle Bin icon to check it's there.

If you've made a mistake in sending a folder to the Recycle Bin, you can still **Restore** it back to it's former place.

Information

You can only recover files sent to the Recycle Bin from the hard drive. If you delete files from a floppy disk, they will not go to the Recycle Bin. The moral of this is, take care when deleting from your floppies!

Saving to the hard disk

Saving a file to your hard disk is the same process that you used to save to a floppy disk in Section 2.

Task 3.10 — Saving file to hard disk

Method

1 Select **Save** from the **File** menu.
2 Select the appropriate drive from the drop down list box.
3 Select the appropriate folder.
4 Click **Open**.
5 Type in the filename.
6 Click **Save**.

→ Practise your skills 1

1 Open your **Word** application.
2 Type in the sentence 'I wish the quick brown dog would lie still.'
3 Save the file to your folder **Section 2** with the filename **Exercise 8**.

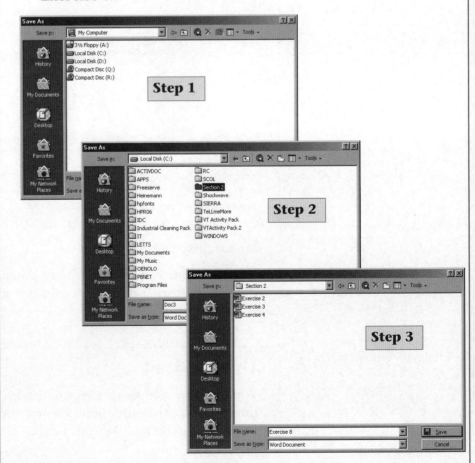

Figure 3.10 Saving to hard disk

Searching for files

As you can imagine, there will be a great many files on your computer and finding the file you want isn't always easy. There are ways to help, however. This can be done using the **Search** button in **My Computer** (Windows ME) or the **Find** option in the **Tools** menu (Windows 98).

Task 3.11 Searching for files

Method

For Windows ME:

1 Open **My Computer**.
2 Click on the **Search** button.
3 Enter the name of the file or folder you want to find in the **Search for files or folders named** box in the left-hand pane.
4 Click on the **Search Now** button.
5 Select the file or folder you want from the list in the right-hand pane.

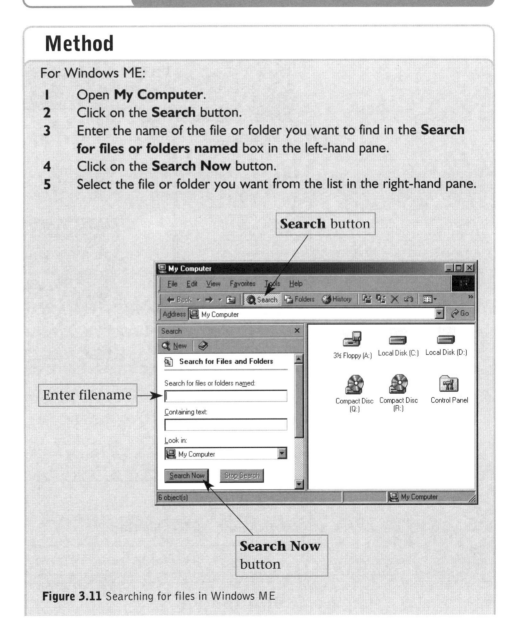

Figure 3.11 Searching for files in Windows ME

Method

For Windows 98:

1   Open **Windows Explorer**.
2   Click on the **Tools** button.
3   Move down to **Find** from the menu.
4   Move the pointer across to **Files or Folders** item and click.
5   Enter the file or folder name in the **Named** box.
6   Click on **Find Now** button.
7   Double click on the file or folder name you want to open it.

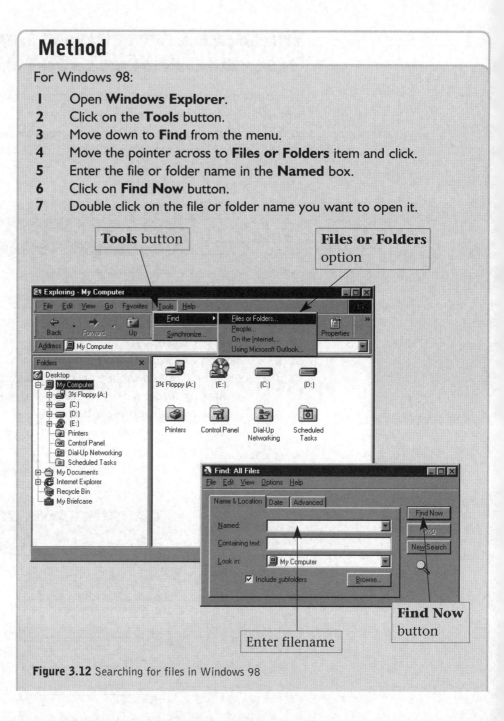

Tools button

Files or Folders option

Find Now button

Enter filename

Figure 3.12 Searching for files in Windows 98

Try it out!

Search for the folder **Section 2**.

Information

These screenshots show the search for a file in the whole of My Computer. You can narrow the search to just a drive, a floppy disk or a CD-ROM (as long as the floppy or CD are in the appropriate drive, of course!) Select the area you want to search from the drop down list box at the side of the **Look in:** box.

Data protection, confidentiality and copyright

Data protection and confidentiality

You will already know the importance of **saving** your work regularly, so that if the unthinkable happens, and your computer crashes, you will still have a copy of your data.

Backing up your data to a floppy disk, CD-ROM, tape or zip disk will also guard against loss of data. Remember that a floppy disk has a special sliding tab which you can slide to **write-protect** your data.

The **Autosave** facility in some programs, such as Microsoft Word, will keep a copy of your data saved – even if you forget to do so!

Making sure your **virus checker** is updated regularly will also prevent loss of data.

Power cuts can cause a loss of the working memory of your computer, which means the work you were in the middle of doing has been lost. This isn't so bad *if* you have remembered to save your work regularly, but it doesn't really do the computer much good. You will remember the importance of shutting down your computer properly? A power cut isn't so careful, and it's the same as switching your computer off at the mains. You can buy a **UPS** (Un-interruptible Power Supply) to protect your computer in case of a power cut. A UPS has batteries which will give you just enough time to save your work and shut down your computer properly.

You can **password-protect** both your files and your computer. If the computer is password-protected, it means that you have to type in your own password to **log on** to the computer. This keeps your files and data safe from other users. In fact, if you are using a computer attached to a network, you may well have your own password already to access the computer. Files can be password-protected too, to make sure that only you can read them if they are private or confidential. You should always keep your password secret and choose something that isn't easy to guess – not your name, for example, or even your favourite football team!

You can also use a special utility called **data encryption.** This will turn your data into code, and a key to the code is needed to make the data readable again.

Data Protection Act

The increasing use of computers to store information about people and their lives caused great concern that all this information could be misused. So the government passed the **Data Protection Act** in 1984. This was updated in the **Data Protection Act 1998**. This protects us all from misuse of personal information and makes those people who gather the information take care of how and why it is used. They also have to make sure it is secure and cannot be used by anyone else for the wrong purposes.

Personal data is kept by many organisations for different reasons, e.g. tax offices, hospital records, personnel departments, banks and building societies. Most of this data will be kept securely, and details shouldn't be available to other people. There are exceptions, such as the police, who are allowed access to such records on occasion.

There are eight principles in the Data Protection Act which ensure that data must be:

- Fairly and lawfully processed
- Processed for limited purposes
- Adequate, relevant and not excessive
- Accurate
- Not kept for longer than necessary
- Processed in line with your rights
- Secure
- Not transferred to other countries without adequate protection.

More information about the Data Protection Act can be found at www.dataprotection.gov.uk/index.htm.

Copyright

The law of copyright protects the work of an author or artist. Copyright information cannot be used without asking the author for permission.

Software programs are protected by copyright. It is illegal to copy them without permission and you may have to pay a large fine if you are caught.

→ Practise your skills 2

1 Create a folder on your hard drive and name it **Unit 1**.
2 Open your file **Exercise 8**.
3 Add the word 'now' to the end of the sentence.
4 Save it as **practice 4** in the folder **Unit 1**.

→ Practise your skills 3

1 Copy the files **practice 1** and **practice 2** from your floppy disk to the folder **Unit 1**.
2 Move the file **Exercise 8** from the folder **Section 2** to the folder **Unit 1**.
3 Rename the file **Exercise 8** as **practice 5**.
4 Back up your folder **Unit 1** to your floppy disk.

→ Practise your skills 4

1 Search for the folder **Section 2**.
2 Delete the folder **Section 2**.

→ Practise your skills 5

1 Open your floppy disk drive to show the files and folders now on the disk.
2 Take a screen capture of the disk contents.
3 Open Word.
4 Use the hotkeys to paste the screen capture into your open document.
5 Save the document in the folder **Unit 1** as **practice 6**.
6 Print a copy of the document.
7 Close and exit Word.

→ Check your knowledge 3

1 You would use a password to:
   a protect your computer from viruses
   b keep your work confidential
   c save your work
   d manage your files

2 Which is the odd one out?
   To protect your data you could:
   a back up your data to floppy disk
   b password-protect your files
   c back up your data to a zip disk
   d update your virus checker once a year

3 Which one of the following would be best to use as a password?
   a a combination of letters and numbers
   b your name
   c your date of birth
   d your brother/sister/mum/dad/pet's name

4 The Data Protection Act:
   a allows anybody to have access to your data
   b says that data doesn't need to be kept securely
   c protects your details from misuse by others
   d says that data doesn't need to be accurate

5 Copyright on commercial software means that:
   a you can't copy the programs without permission
   b you can copy the programs
   c you can give a copy to a friend
   d it isn't illegal to copy them

Section 4 | Working with windows

You will learn to

- Use different parts of the desktop
- Identify basic desktop icons and shortcuts
- Change the computer's desktop configuration and desktop display options
- Use the following functions of the desktop window:
  - ☐ Maximise, minimise a window
  - ☐ Restore a window from the taskbar
  - ☐ Make a desktop window taller, shorter, narrower or wider
  - ☐ Move windows on the desktop
  - ☐ Keyboard functions
  - ☐ Switch between programs
  - ☐ Switch between documents
- Identify the computer's basic system information
- Cancel a print job

Having learnt a little about your computer and how to organise and manage your work, it is time to move on to see what happens on your desktop and how to use the windows which display information or documents.

The desktop

You will remember from Section 2 that when you power up your computer and the operating system is loaded your desktop will be displayed, which will look similar to the screen shot below:

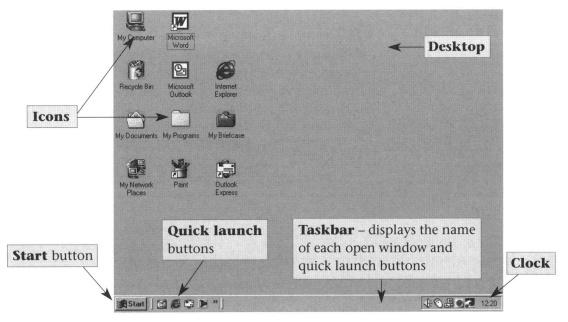

Figure 4.1 Desktop display

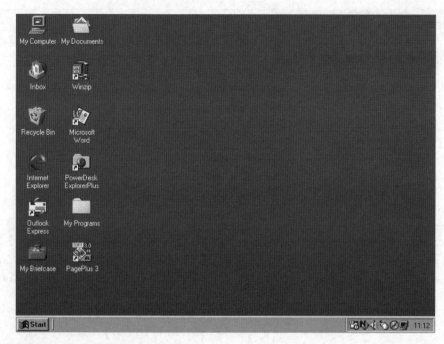

Figure 4.2 Windows 98 desktop

Information

The screen shot in Figure 4.1 was created using Windows ME (Millenium Edition) operating system. If you are using Windows 95 or 98 you may find that your desktop will look slightly different, as in Figure 4.2. Can you spot the differences in the way the icons appear?

Icons

Icons are small pictures or graphics which represent programs, folders or files.

This is a **shortcut** icon to a program – Microsoft Word. A shortcut icon on the desktop is a quick way to access your program instead of going through the **Start** menu. Shortcut icons for your most frequently used programs or files are useful when they are on the desktop. You can tell it's a shortcut by the little arrow in the left-hand corner.

Task 4.1   Creating a shortcut to a program

Method

1	Click on the **Start** button.
2	Find the program **Word** in the programs menu.
3	Click on it with the right mouse button.
4	Select **Send To** from the menu.
5	Select **Desktop (create shortcut)** from the menu.

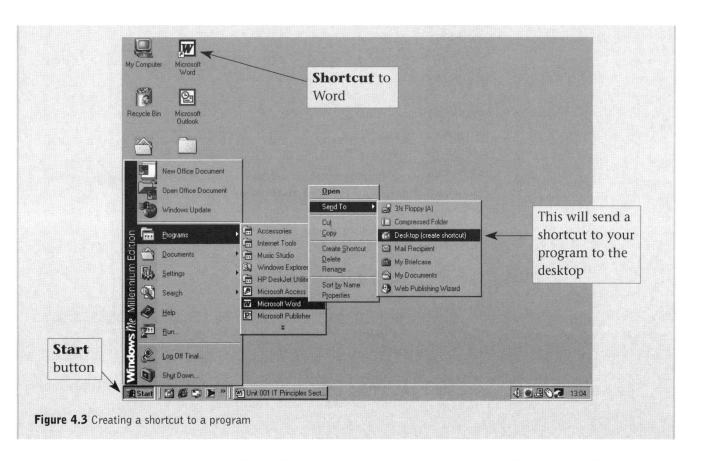

Figure 4.3 Creating a shortcut to a program

Task 4.2 | Creating a shortcut to a file

Method

1	Open **My Computer** or **Windows Explorer**.
2	Find the appropriate file.
3	Click on it with the right mouse button.
4	Select **Send To** from the menu.
5	Select **Desktop (create shortcut)** from the menu.

 This is a **folder** icon.

 This is an example of a **file** icon. The icon above the filename tells you what type of file it is. This is a Word file.

Some of the icons on your desktop may be:

 My Computer – this will allow you to see the files and programs on your computer.

 Recycle Bin – this will allow you to see which files have been deleted and restore them if you want to.

Internet Explorer – this will allow you to access the Internet.

 Outlook Express – this will allow you to access your e-mail.

Some of the icons in **My Computer** may be:

 Floppy disk drive A:

 Hard disk drive C:

 Compact disc drive (in this case Q:)

 Control Panel – this allows you to access the settings and information for your computer.

Information

If you click on any file, folder or other icon with the right mouse button, you will be able to select **Properties** from the menu. This will tell you more information about the file, folder, program etc.

Try it out!

- Open **My Computer**.
- Find your file **Exercise 2**.
- Right mouse click on the file.
- Select **Properties** from the pop-up menu.
- Note down the following properties of your file (you may have to click on the tabs along the top of the box to find out all the information):
  - ☐ Type of document
  - ☐ Its location
  - ☐ The date it was created
  - ☐ How many words are in the document.

→ Check your knowledge 1

1 Icons are:
   a small graphics which can only represent programs
   b small graphics which can only represent files
   c small graphics which can represent programs, files or folders
   d small graphics which can only represent files or folders

2 Internet Explorer will allow you to:
   a access the Internet   **b** access your word processor
   c access your deleted files   **d** access your floppy disk drive

3 The Files or Folder Properties box will tell you:
   a what the time is   **b** what the date is
   c the type of document   **d** what type of computer you are using

Changing the desktop properties

You can change many of the properties on your desktop.

Date and time

The time is displayed in the far right corner of the taskbar. If you hold your mouse pointer over this clock, the date will appear.

Usually, computers keep reasonable time, but you may have to alter it now and again to keep it spot on the right time.

Task 4.3	Changing date and time

Method

1   Double click on the **Clock** icon.
2   The **Date/Time Properties** box appears.
3   Click in the appropriate boxes to change the date and time as necessary.
4   Click on **Apply**.
5   Click on **OK**.

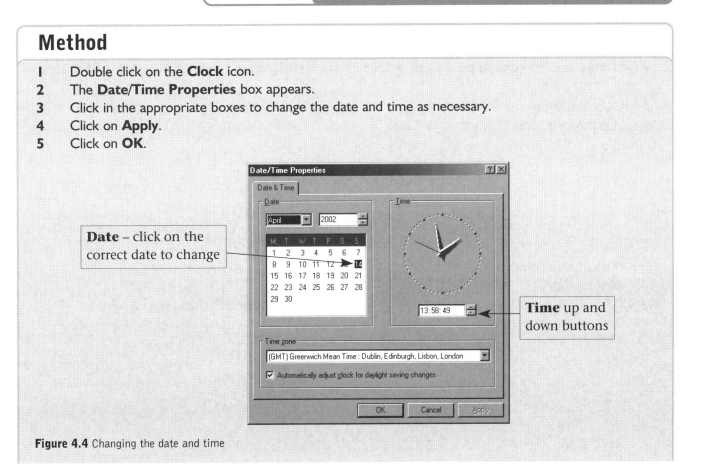

Figure 4.4 Changing the date and time

Display options

You can change the way your desktop looks by using the **Display Properties** dialogue box.

Task 4.4	Changing the appearance of the desktop

Method

1   Using right mouse, click in a blank part of your desktop.
2   A **Display Properties** dialogue box will appear.

From here you can click on the tabs and change the appearance of your desktop. You can change:

- **Background** – this allows you to change the colour and appearance of your desktop. You could change the wallpaper to a picture or a pattern.
- **Screen saver** – this allows you to select different effects for screen savers. A screen saver will be displayed when you have left your computer for a while. You can change the time settings for the screen saver to be activated.
- **Appearance** – from here you can choose a variety of different colour schemes for your desktop and windows. Some are very bright indeed! Others can be set to use large fonts which would be helpful for someone with visual difficulties.
- **Web** – this allows you to view your desktop as a web page.
- **Effects** – changing some of your icons and how they are viewed could be done from here. Large icons may be helpful for some people to enable them to identify what they are representing.
- **Settings** – you can change the number of colours used in the display as well as the number of pixels in the screen area.

3   Click on **Apply**.
4   **Click on** OK.

If you find that you don't want to change anything after all, simply click on **Cancel**.

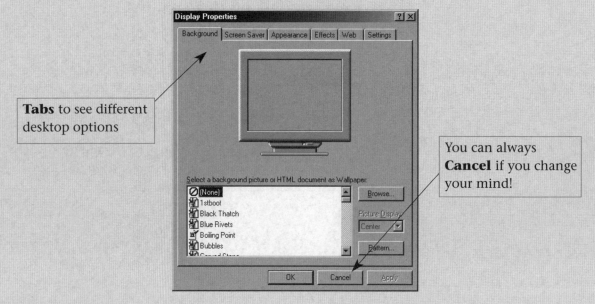

Figure 4.5 Display Properties dialogue box

Try it out!

Open the Display Properties dialogue box and find out the following:

1 How many different **wallpapers** do you have to choose from on your computer?

2 What shape and colour are the **3D Flying Objects** in the screen saver of the same name?

3 How would you describe the colours in the **Scheme–Pumpkin (large)**?

4 What are the settings for **Colors** (the American spelling!) and the **pixels** for the screen area?

Sound settings

Changing the sound settings might be useful if you were playing a music CD in your CR-ROM drive.

Task 4.5 — Changing sound settings

Method

1 Double click on the **Volume** icon 🔊 on the taskbar.
2 The **Volume Control** panel appears.
3 Move the sliders up and down to change the volume.
4 Close the panel.

Arranging desktop icons

Task 4.6 — Arranging your desktop icons

Method 1

1 Select the icon and hold down the mouse button.
2 Drag the icon to its new place.

Method 2

1 Using right mouse, click in a blank area of the desktop.
2 Select **Arrange Icons** from the pop-up menu.
3 Select the way you would like to arrange your icons. **Auto Arrange** is very useful as it will line them up for you in neat rows!

Figure 4.6 Arranging desktop icons

→ **Check your knowledge 2**

1 Which is the odd one out?
   The Display Properties dialogue box will allow you to:
   a change your wallpaper
   b change your time and date
   c change your screen saver
   d change the colour scheme

2 Auto Arrange will:
   a arrange your icons by name
   b arrange your icons by size
   c arrange your icons for you
   d arrange your icons in date order

Using window functions

A **window** is a rectangular area on your desktop which displays documents or applications you have open. You have already met quite a few windows in the last three sections, but there are many other functions which can be used with a desktop window.

First, a recap on the parts of a window:

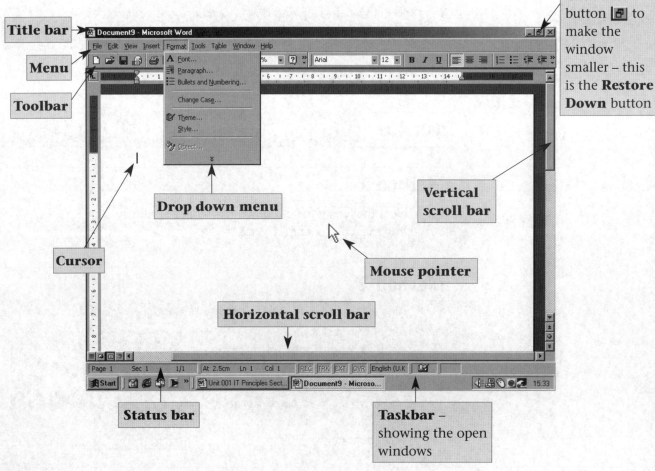

Figure 4.7 Parts of a window

Parts of the document window

- **Title bar** This shows the name of the document (Document 9, in this case) and the program being used (Microsoft Word).
- **Menu bar** This shows the menu names. Any of these menu items can be selected using the mouse or keyboard. A drop down menu will appear which will give you more options to choose from. You may need to hold your mouse pointer over the double arrows at the bottom of the drop down menu until all items are displayed, as only the most recently used items are shown when the menu first drops down.

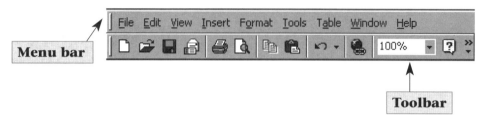

Figure 4.8 Standard toolbar

- **Toolbar** There are different toolbars for different purposes. Figure 4.8 is the **Standard toolbar**, where many of the most used functions are located, such as **Print** and **Save**. These are buttons you can click on to choose the function shown by the picture.

Try it out!

- If you hold your mouse pointer over the toolbar buttons, a **ToolTip** will appear, giving a brief explanation about the button.
- Using the picture below, identify what the different buttons are and write them in the boxes.

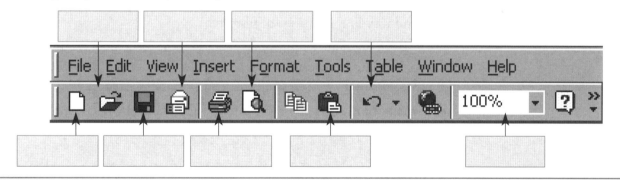

- **Cursor** This flashing bar shows where your text will be placed when you type into the document.
- **Scroll bars** You can use these to move your view of the document up or down and side to side. This will let you see text that isn't showing in the window.
- **Mouse pointer** This will move as you move the mouse and let you select items in the window. There are many designs for mouse pointers – this is the default (set up when first installed).
- **Minimise button** This will let you reduce your application to a button on the taskbar. This is useful if you have many windows open at the same time. To restore your window, simply click on the button on the taskbar.

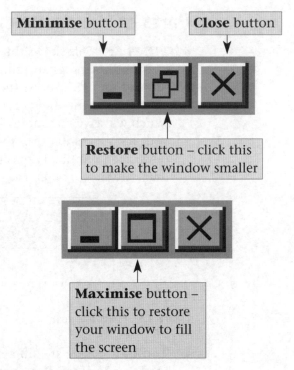

Figure 4.9 Window control buttons

- **Maximise/Restore button** Toggle these buttons to fill the screen or to make the window smaller. This is useful if you want to reduce your window to find something on the desktop.
- **Close button** Clicking this closes your document and exits the application. This is quite a bit quicker than using the menus, but make sure you save your work before you use it!
- **Taskbar** This shows the windows you have open. If you have **minimised** them onto the taskbar, simply click on the title of the window you want to see to restore it.

    If you have your windows open on screen you can click on the appropriate **taskbar** button to **toggle** (move from one to the other) between them.

- **Status bar** This gives you information about the page numbers, and the position of the cursor on the screen.

Moving windows

You can move and arrange your open windows by clicking and holding down the left mouse button on the title bar and moving the window to where you would like it to be. This is called **dragging**. Release the mouse button when you have the window in place. As you **drag** the window, you will see an outline moving with your mouse pointer. The rest of the window will catch up to the outline when you release the mouse button.

> **Information**
>
> You cannot move maximised windows.

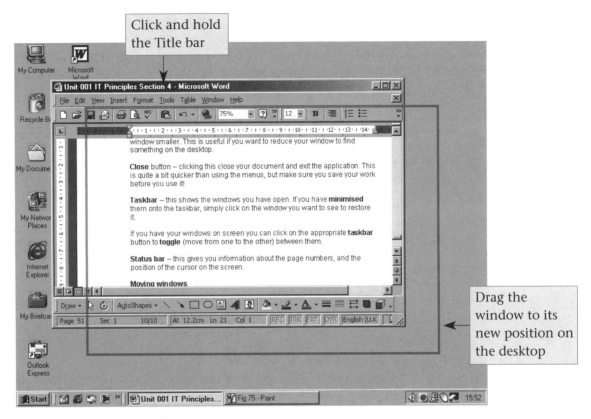

Figure 4.10 Dragging a window to a new position

Sizing windows

You can change the shape of a window by moving your mouse pointer to the edge of the window. The pointer will change into a **double-headed arrow** shape. Hold down the left mouse button and drag the window to the shape you require.

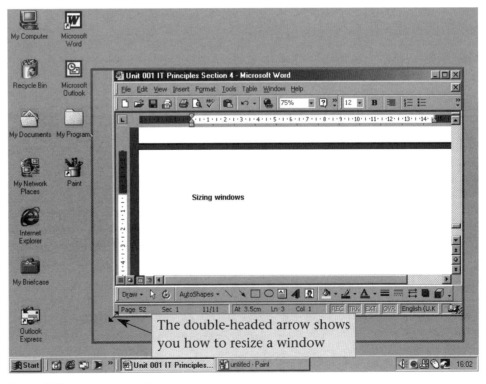

Figure 4.11 Resizing a window

Using this method you can make windows taller, shorter, narrower or wider. It can be very useful if you have a few applications open and you want to place them side by side so that you can view them at the same time. You would simply resize each window so that they would fit into the screen.

As you **drag** the window, you will see an outline moving with your mouse pointer. The rest of the window will catch up to the outline when you release the mouse button.

Keyboard functions

Using a combination of keys on the keyboard, as you have already found out, can help speed up some of the tasks you need to do. It will take some practice to get really comfortable with them, but it will be well worth the effort. Try listing some of those you find really useful, and remember to use them instead of other methods of doing the same task.

You will now learn some more useful keyboard functions.

Switching between programs

We have seen that you can use the buttons on the taskbar to switch between open programs, but, as with many of the other functions, there is another way of using the keyboard alone.

Task 4.7	Switching between programs

Method

1   Hold down the **Alt** key on the keyboard (usually placed just under the letter keys).

2   Press the **Tab** key.

3   A small window appears with the icons of all the open folders and applications.
4   As you hold down the **Alt** key, you can cycle through the icons in the window.
5   When you reach the icon you want to select, release both the keys and the selected window is restored and active on your desktop.

Switching between documents

If you have an application open with more than one document on the go – perhaps you have two letters which you are writing, but not quite finished – it would be handy to be able to go from one document to the other quickly. This can be done with the help of yet another keyboard combination.

Method

1. Hold down the **Alt** key.
2. Press the **W** key on the keyboard.
3. A drop down menu will appear from the **Window** button on the **Menu bar**.
4. Select from the list of documents the one you want to go to. The one that is currently on view will have a tick by it.

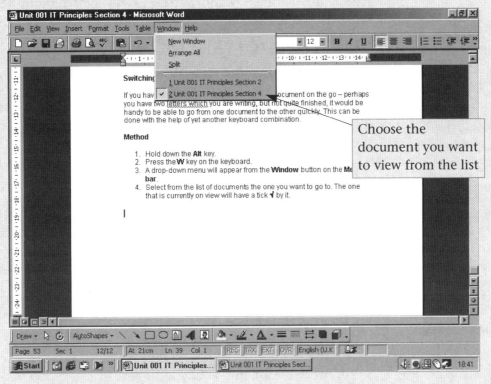

Choose the document you want to view from the list

Figure 4.12 Switching to view another document

Other useful keyboard functions

In this group of keys are:

- **Insert key** This will allow you to type over and replace text instead of having to delete it first.
- **Delete key** This deletes letters in front of the cursor.
- **Home key** This moves the cursor to the beginning of the line.
- **End key** This moves the cursor to the end of the line.
- **Page Up** This moves one screen up.
- **Page Down** This moves one screen down.

If you use the **Ctrl key** with some of these keys, you can move around your document even more:

Ctrl + Home	moves to the beginning of the document
Ctrl + End	moves to the end of the document

| **Ctrl + Page Up** | moves to the top of the previous page |
| **Ctrl + Page Down** | moves to the top of the next page. |

 The **Number Lock key** will allow you to use the smaller numeric pad on the right of the keyboard. A small light on the keyboard usually indicates if the Number Lock is on.

 The **F1 key** will call up the **Help** files.

If the unexpected happens, and the computer crashes so that you can't do anything in your open window, there are keyboard options which might just help:

Ctrl + Alt + Delete will allow you to end a task.

The **Windows key**, which is at the bottom left side of the keyboard with a picture of the Microsoft Windows logo 🪟, will bring up the **Start** menu and allow you to shut down the computer. (**Note**: not all keyboards will have this key.)

Try it out!

Using the **Help** files, find the information on 'Keys for editing and moving text and graphics'. Print out a copy for yourself to use as reference.

→ Check your knowledge 3

1   The status bar tells you:
   a what time it is
   b what windows you have open
   c information about page numbers
   d what the volume setting is

2   You can resize windows when the pointer changes to:
   a a hand
   b a single-headed arrow
   c a double-headed arrow
   d a dotted line

3   To switch between open programs you would use the key combination:
   a Alt + Tab
   b Alt + V
   c Ctrl + Tab
   d Shift + Tab

The computer's basic system information

You can use the **Control Panel** to find out about many of the settings on your computer. You can also alter computer settings using **Control Panel**.

Method

1   Click on the **Start** button.
2   Move the mouse pointer up to **Settings** and select **Control Panel** from the next menu.
3   From the open **Control Panel** window, double click on the **System** icon.
4   Select the tabs to find out the information you need.

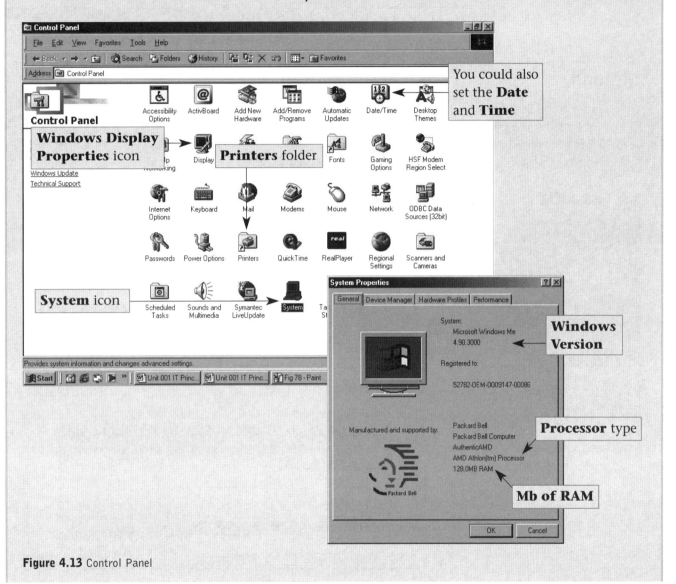

Figure 4.13 Control Panel

Try it out!

Access your **System** properties information and note down:

1   the Windows version you are using
2   the processor type in your machine
3   how many megabytes of RAM your machine has.

Cancelling a print job

Documents that are waiting to be printed are stored in a **print queue**. You can take a look at the print queue to see a list of the documents waiting to be printed and the order in which they will be printed.

Task 4.10   Viewing the print queue

Method

1   Click on the **Start** button.
2   Move the mouse pointer up to **Settings**.
3   Select **Printers** from the menu which appears.
4   Double click on the printer icon for the printer you are using.

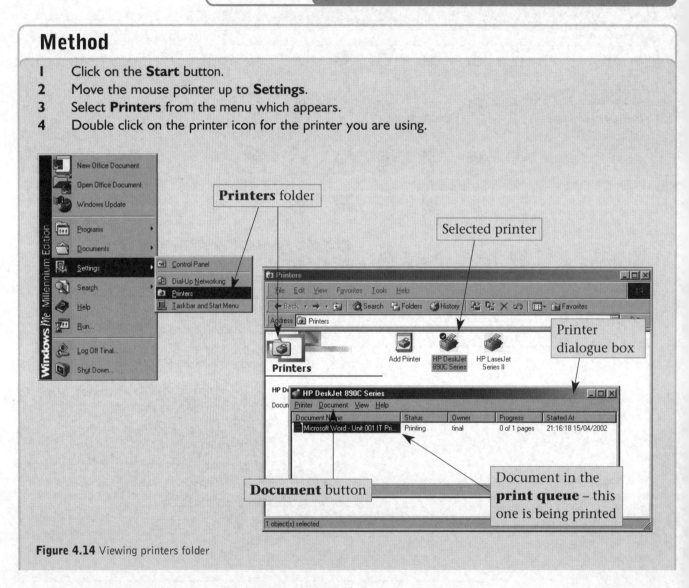

Figure 4.14 Viewing printers folder

Pausing or cancelling a print job

If you suddenly realise that you've made a mistake sending your document to be printed, you can either pause the printer (while you think what to do!) or cancel it. You may find that there will be a little delay in the response from the printer because it is already acting on instructions from the computer and will complete the printing of the data stored in its memory. A partly printed document could be the result!

Method

I	Select **Document** on the printers dialogue box menu bar.
2	Select **Pause** or **Cancel** from the drop down menu.

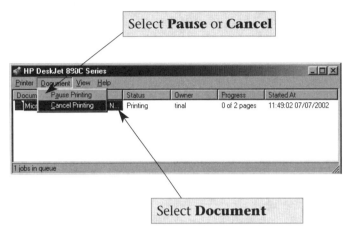

Figure 4.15 Printers dialogue box

→ Practise your skills 1

1 Open **My Computer** or **Windows Explorer**.

2 Find the file **practice 5** on your floppy disk.

3 Note down the properties of the file.

4 Create a shortcut to your desktop for the file.

5 Arrange the icons on your desktop so that your new shortcut icon is in the top right-hand corner.

6 Delete the shortcut icon.

→ Practise your skills 2

1 Create a folder on your desktop called **Unit 1**.

2 Create shortcuts on your desktop for the files **practice 1, 2, 3** and **4** from your floppy disk.

3 Move the shortcuts for the four files into your folder **Unit 1**.

4 Open your folder and **Auto Arrange** your icons.

5 Take a screen shot of your open folder and paste it into a new Word document.

6 Print out a copy of the document.

7 Save your file as **practice 7** in your folder **Unit 1** on your hard drive, and exit Word.

8 Close your folder and move it to the bottom right-hand corner of your screen.

→ Practise your skills 3

1 Open the files **practice 1, 2, 3** and **4**.

2 Arrange the windows to fit into your desktop as shown in the screen shot below.

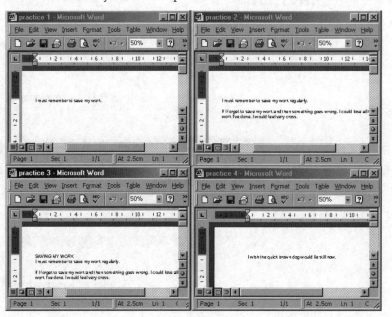

Figure 4.16

3 Take a screen shot of your window and paste it into a new Word document.

4 Print a copy of the document.

5 Save the file as **practice 8** in your folder **Unit 1** on your hard drive, and exit Word.

6 Minimise all windows to the taskbar.

7 Restore the files **practice 1** and **practice 2** onto your desktop.

8 Place the windows side by side as shown in the screen shot below.

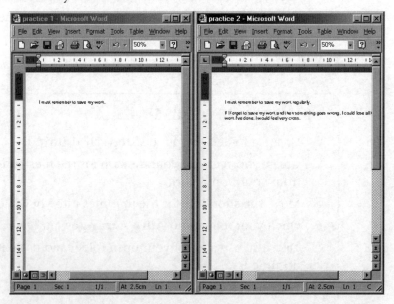

Figure 4.17

9 Take a screen shot of your window and paste it into a new Word document.

10 Print a copy of the document.

11 Save the file as **practice 9** in your folder **Unit 1** on your hard drive, and exit Word.

12 Close all open windows.

→ Practise your skills 4

1 Open the **Printers** folder and note the printers shown.

2 Open the **Settings** folder.

3 Access the **System** dialogue box.

4 Arrange the two windows side by side on the desktop.

5 Take a screen shot of your window and paste it into a new Word document.

6 Print a copy of the document.

7 Save the file as **practice 10** in your folder **Unit 1** on your hard drive, and exit Word.

8 Close all open windows.

9 Shut down the computer.

Networking

Computer networks

A computer which is not connected to any other computer is called a **standalone** machine. This is fine if you're just working on your own, at home perhaps, but if you want to get information to another person, you would have to print it out or save it to a floppy disk (but remember the risk of virus infection if you use floppy disks that have been used in a lot of different computers). That could take up precious time and energy. Imagine if you had to do that in a big organisation. If the computers are connected together by means of cables, you could exchange information much more easily. This is called a **network**.

Computer networks can be found in many organisations, large and small. There are different ways to connect the computers together and often the computers will be connected to a large computer called a **server.** This will have more processing power and storage space on its hard drive – it may even have several hard drives to store all the information needed for a large organisation.

The latest technology now allows computers to be joined without cables in a **wireless network**. It may well be some time before this is in general use in businesses, but many home computer users are using wireless networking to connect their computer equipment and peripherals.

Using a network means that many people in the organisation can share software, peripherals such as printers, and information. Networks can be used within one building or can stretch across the globe.

Local area networks

Local area networks (**LANs**) are confined to a small area, often just a single building. How the network is set up will depend on the needs of the organisation. A typical small LAN is shown in Figure 5.1. Here three workstations can access centrally held data on the server, and share the laser printer.

A LAN allows users to send messages to each other using a local **electronic mail system,** more often called **e-mail**.

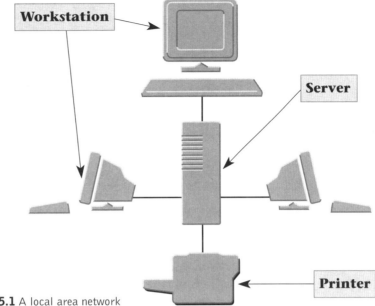

Figure 5.1 A local area network

Wide area networks

Wide area networks (**WANs**) consist of terminals and computer equipment connected over a much larger area. Using WANs, computers can be connected to each other in cities across a country or across continents via telecommunication links, such as your own phone line at home, to enable them to share data and information almost instantaneously.

Global network

The **Internet** is a **global network**. It connects users over the world and is used to find and exchange information as well as to send and receive e-mails. Connecting to this global network at home will be different from logging on to your workplace network. At home, you will probably use your phone line and modem to connect to the Internet to send and receive emails.

Network operating software

Just as a standalone computer needs software to drive it, so a network also needs an operating system to run it. There are several network operating systems available developed, for example by Novel and UNIX as well as Microsoft.

The **network operating system** will have to cope with the demands of many computers and be able to supply the services each user needs. It will control how the network printer is used and place all documents sent to the printer in an orderly queue to be printed in turn. Handling all the internal e-mails passing from person to person is another of its functions, and it will store all the details about who is logged on to the system and what they are doing.

Logging on to access a network

Specific parts of the program will be designed to control access to the data and information stored on the server. Every user will be allowed to access only certain parts of the data available, and this will be controlled centrally by the operating system. Users will have **passwords** which they will enter when they **log on** to the system to be able to access programs and data. The operating system will check that the password is correct and then allow the user to begin using the software and information available to them. A typical log on screen is shown below.

Figure 5.2 A log on screen

The access users will be allowed to the data on the network is set by the network administrator and will depend on the tasks that they will have to do. This is called **access rights**. For example, an accounts clerk won't need to have access to everyone's personal details to keep track of the invoices coming into the organisation. In a college, students will have access rights to a part of the network which has been allocated to them and to the software which their rights allow them to use. A tutor, on the other hand, will have rights to much more data on the network, such as exam papers.

Try it out!

1 Switch on your computer.
2 **Log on** to the network using your password.

Using a network

Having logged on to the network, using the software is exactly the same as for a standalone machine. The only differences may be using a networked printer or other peripherals, or having to save work to a specific area of the network. You may have to wait that bit longer to get the printouts if there are several other people trying to print work at the same time.

Information: Rights to files

There are different rights which can be given to network users. Some rights will allow users to change the data in a file, other rights will not. The different levels of access rights are:

- **Read** – allows the user to read the files in a particular directory.
- **Write** – allows the user to change the data in a particular directory.
- **Create** – allows the user to create new files, directories and subdirectories.
- **Delete** – allows the user to delete certain files and directories.
- **Modify** – allows the user to rename directories and files.
- **Copy** – allows the user to copy work from one area to another.

Displaying files to which access is provided

In the screen shots below a student at college is finding a file called Chinese signs.doc to complete a key skills activity. The file has been placed in the student area of the network by the tutor.

The address of the file is:

Applicat on 'Efloor_1'[S]/Students/shared/key skills/Assessment Activities/ Chinese signs.doc

Each of the folders or subdirectories the student has to navigate is separated by a forward slash (/). See if you can follow these directions on the diagrams.

> ## Information
>
> The icon for a network drive looks a little different to the ones which you have met in previous sections. Look carefully at the screen shots to spot this icon.

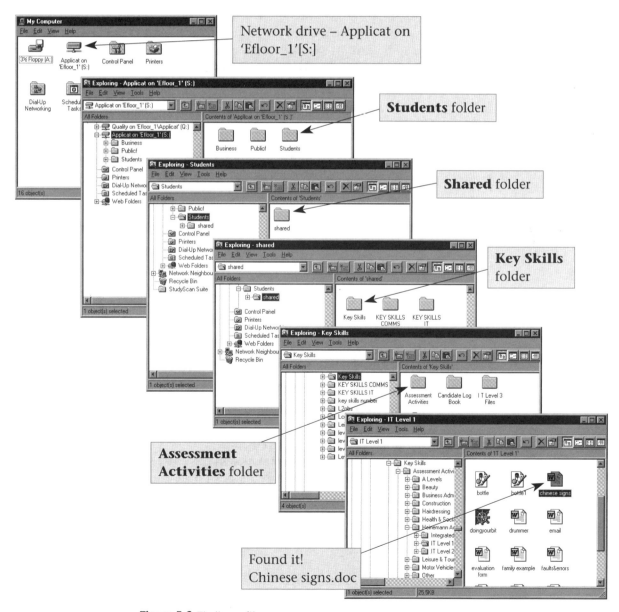

Figure 5.3 Finding a file

Although students can access and open the file to use for the activity, they can't change the information in the file because they don't have the rights to do so. If they need to change the data they will have to copy the file to a floppy disk before they can begin (assuming the rights to copy have been allowed!)

Selecting, opening, editing and saving a shared file

To find a file, open it, edit it and save it on a network is very much like doing those same tasks on a standalone computer.

Quite often on a network you may not have access to the hard drive of the computer you are using. A hard drive might soon get filled up if work was being saved there all the time, not to mention that the network administrator, who looks after the network, would not be able to keep track of everything that was going on. This means that you would need to find your file on the network drive to which you have access. The storage space on a server may well be divided into many network drives, each one given a different letter or name. If you open **My Computer**, the drive you can access may be the only one shown, although there will be more which other people can use. As you can see in the screen shot, the only network drive shown is the **Applicat on 'Efloor_1'(S:)** drive.

Applicat on 'Efloor_1'(S:) drive

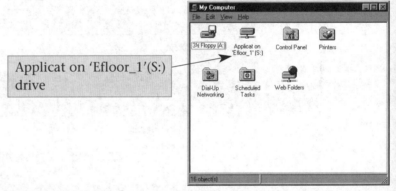

Figure 5.4 A network drive

| Task 5.1 | Loading a shared file |

Method

1   Open your application.
2   Select the **Open** option in the **File** menu.
3   Select the appropriate drive from the drop down drive list box.
4   Navigate the folders on the drive to find the file you need.
5   **Select** the file you need.
6   Click **Open**.

Once your file is open, you can **edit** (change) it, perhaps by adding information or even removing information which you no longer want to include. Having made your changes, you can **save** your file.

Method 1

1   Select the **Save** option in the **File** menu.
2   Make sure that the drive and filename are correct.
3   Click on **Save**.

Method 2

I   Click on the **Save** icon 💾 on the toolbar.

Try it out!

1   Load **Word**.
2   Open your file **Lazy dog** from your floppy disk.
3   Delete the word 'sometimes' and add the word 'today' to the end of the sentence.
4   **Save** your file with the filename **Lazy dog today** to your area of the network.
5   **Save** your file again.
6   Close and **Exit** Word.

Printing your file

It is not uncommon to have a number of computers on a network sharing one printer. It is obviously cheaper to have one printer for several computer users than for each user to have a printer of their own. It does mean that you may have to wait in a queue to have your file printed out. The network software will handle this queue, and each file sent to the printer will be put into the queue in sequence. The screen shot below shows a number of documents waiting to be printed.

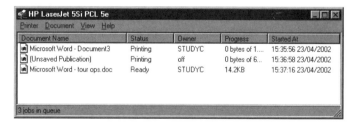

Figure 5.5 Documents in a print queue

Sometimes, more than one printer may be attached to a network, and you will need to choose the printer you want to send your document to before you click the **Print** button. The screen shot in Figure 5.6 shows a choice of two printers. The Deskjet might be used if a colour print was required, but the Laserjet could be used for high quality black and white copies.

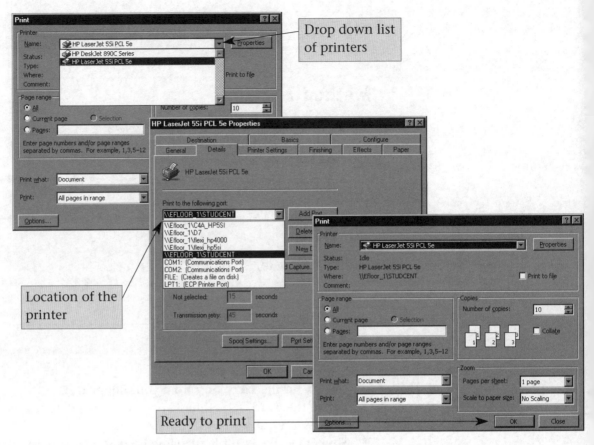

Figure 5.6 Choosing a printer

Task 5.3 — Using a printer attached to a network

Method

1   Select **Print** from the **File** menu.
2   Select the **printer** from the drop down list box.
3   Select any options you want, such as landscape or portrait.
4   Click on **OK**.

Information

You can view the print queue by clicking on the **printer** icon on the taskbar.

Try it out!

1   Load **Word**.
2   **Open** your file **Lazy dog today**.
3   **Send** your document to the network printer.
4   **View** the network printer queue.
5   Close and **Exit** Word.

Logging off a network

When you have completed your work you can't just leave your computer logged on, because this would allow other people to access your files. You will have to choose whether to **log off** the network or **shut down** the computer. If you log off the network, the operating system will know that you are no longer using the computer and will then allow someone else to log on to the machine. They will need their own password to do this, just as you did. If you shut down the computer, you will need to switch it on again and log on the next time you want to use it.

Task 5.4	Logging off a network

Method

I   Click the **Start** button.
2   Select the **Close all programs and log on as a different user** option from the menu or drop down list box.
Your dialogue box to log off may look similar to the one shown here.

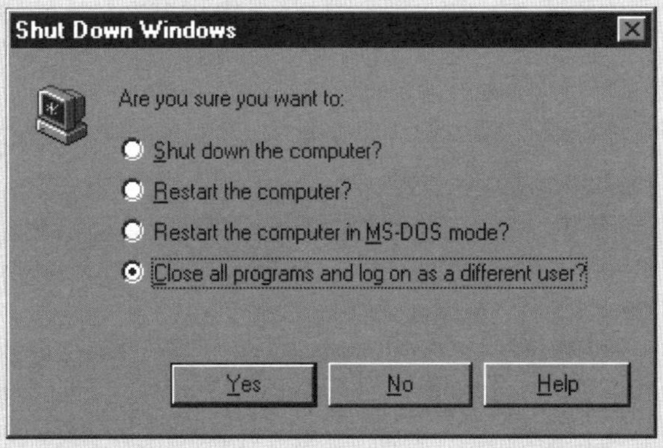

Figure 5.7 Shut Down dialogue box

→ **Check your knowledge 1**

1   A computer which is not connected to another computer is a:
   a   terminal
   b   standalone machine
   c   networked
   d   server

2   A LAN is *best* described as a:
   a   global network
   b   wide area network
   c   network operating system
   d   network confined to a small area

3   When logging on to a network the password is checked by:
   a   the disk operating system
   b   the network operating system
   c   the software operating system
   d   the global operating system

4   To change data in a file you have the rights to:
   a   read the file
   b   modify the file
   c   delete the file
   d   copy the file

E-mail

One of the quickest ways of communicating with others on a network is to use e-mail. This is a method of sending letters, memos, pictures and sounds from one computer to another. If you are at home, you may use a modem to connect to your phone line so that you can send e-mails to anywhere in the world and receive e-mails in reply. This is often quicker than 'snail mail' (the name sometimes used for the traditional postal system) and, usually, just for the cost of a local phone call.

If you are on a network, you will be able to send messages to other people in your organisation as well as sending them to people outside the network through a phone line or ISDN (Integrated Services Digital Network) connection. Whether you are sending or receiving e-mails internally or externally you will need to have e-mail software, such as Microsoft **Outlook Express**, installed on your computer or network.

To send an e-mail to someone, you will need to know their e-mail address. This is a unique address that will look something like the one shown below:

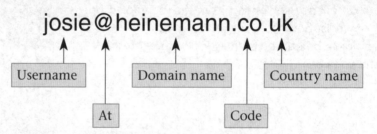

Figure 5.8 A unique e-mail address

- **Username** – the name or nickname of the person.
- **Domain name** – the unique address of the computer. This has three main sections that tell you where the computer is:
    - ☐ **heinemann** – the organisation where the user works or the **Internet Service Provider's** name
    - ☐ **co** – this tells you the type of organisation
    - ☐ **uk** – this tells you the country.

Information

Internet Service Providers (ISP) and Online Services provide a gateway to the Internet. This would usually be the way you would access the Internet from a home computer via your phone line. Many ISPs and Online Services will provide this service for a small monthly fee.

There are several types of organisations and you can tell from the e-mail address which type it is:

ac	an academic organisation
co or **com**	a commercial organisation
edu	an educational institution
gov	a government body
net	an organisation involved in running the Net
org	a non-profit-making organisation

To start your **e-mail** software, double click on the **Outlook Express** icon, which will be on your desktop, or click the icon on the taskbar or in the programs menu (if you have a different e-mail package, you will need to open this program instead).

Outlook Express

Information

The following screen shots use **Outlook Express**, but, although the windows might look slightly different if you are using another e-mail package, the procedures for using your system will be much the same.

You will find a window similar to the one shown below:

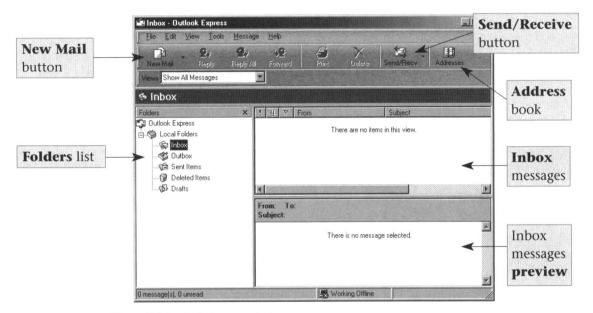

Figure 5.9 Outlook Express window

In the folders list you will have:

* **Inbox** – where the messages you receive are stored.
* **Outbox** – where messages you are sending are stored.
* **Sent Items** – this folder stores the messages you have sent.
* **Deleted Items** – where any messages you have deleted are stored.
* **Drafts** – where messages you are still working on are stored.

If you click on a folder, it will show you all the messages stored inside it.

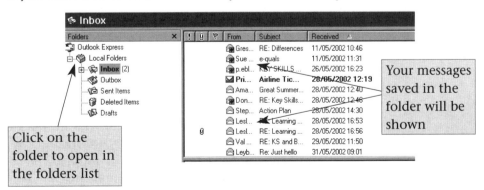

Figure 5.10 An open folder

Method

1 Click on the **New Mail** button

2 The **New Message** window will appear.
3 Click in the **To:** box, and type in the e-mail address of the person you are sending the message to.
4 Click in the **Subject:** box, and type in a word or short sentence to indicate what the message is about.
5 Click in the message section underneath, and type in your message.

6 Click on the **Send** button

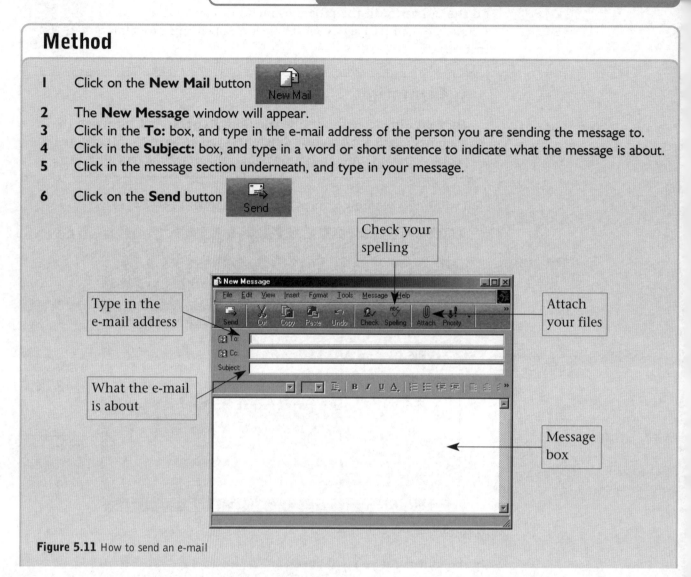

Figure 5.11 How to send an e-mail

Information

Check your typing carefully – make sure you haven't left any spaces in the address or left out any of the full stops.

Information

You can use the spellchecking button to check that you haven't made any spelling errors.

If you are using an internal network, your message will be sent straight away. This will also happen if your network has a permanent connection to the phone system or to an ISDN line. A copy of the message will be placed in your **Sent Items** folder. If you have prepared your message **off-line** (not connected) your message will be place in your **Outbox** folder. It will remain there until you connect to your ISP and click on the **Send and Receive All** button.

Method

I   Click on the **Send and Receive All** button.
2   Any incoming messages will be placed in your **Inbox** folder.
3   Click on the **Inbox** folder.
4   Select the new message to read it.

Using an address book

On a network, you will probably find your organisation address list if you

click on the **Addresses** button   You can use this list to select a

name to be entered in the **To:** box of a **New Message** to save you having to
type it in yourself!

You can also store your most used addresses in the Address Book.

If you need a copy of your e-mail, you can print out a copy using the **Print**
option in the **File** menu or the **Print** button on the toolbar.

→ Practise your skills 1

1   Open your e-mail program.
2   Enter the e-mail address of someone within your organisation who is
    aware that you will be sending this e-mail.
3   Enter 'Just Learning' in the **Subject** box.
4   Enter this message: 'I'm learning to use e-mail – please will you reply to
    me.'
5   **Send** the message. (If you are working off-line you will need to
    connect to your ISP.)
6   Close your e-mail program.

→ Practise your skills 2

1   Open your e-mail program.
2   Check to see if you have any new mail.
3   Read your new mail.
4   Print out a copy.
5   Close your e-mail program.

Using e-mail attachments

You can **attach** files and documents to your e-mail, which makes it very
useful if you want to get your documents to someone more quickly (and
often more cheaply) than snail mail.

Method

1   Load your e-mail program.
2   Click on the **New Message** button on the toolbar.
3   Enter the e-mail address, the subject and your message.
4   Click on the **Attach File** button on the toolbar.
5   The **Insert Attachment** window appears.
6   Select the drive where the file you wish to send has been saved.
7   Click on the file, so that it appears in the **Filename** box.
8   Click on **Attach**.
9   Your file will be shown in the **Attach:** box of your message.
10   **Send** the e-mail.

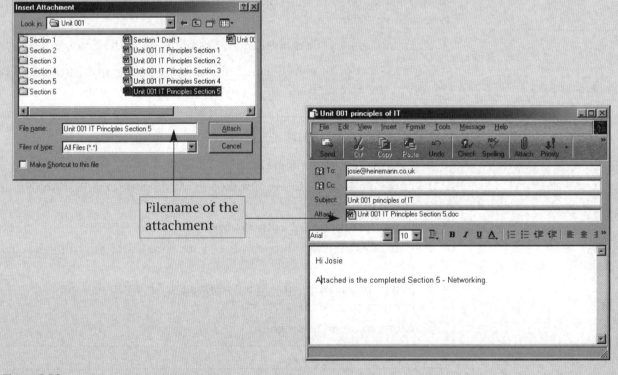

Figure 5.12 Attaching a document to an e-mail

E-mails can also be sent to you with an attachment. You will need to take great care opening any such files you receive as they can carry viruses. It is important to scan any e-mail attachment with a virus checker before you open it.

Other functions of e-mail

- You can send a reply to any e-mail you receive by using the **Reply** button on the toolbar.
- You can forward messages you have received to another person using the **Forward** button.
- You can send one message to several people at the same time by entering all the e-mail addresses in the **To:** box. The addresses would be separated by semicolons.

- If you want to send a copy of your e-mail to someone else, you can use the **Cc:** box to enter the appropriate e-mail address.
- You can keep your folders tidy by **deleting** messages that you no longer need – just like you would do with paper documents.

Video conferencing

Video conferencing is a way that people in many different parts of the country or the world can talk to each other without leaving their home or office. Of course, you have been able to talk to people anywhere in the world using your telephone connection for many years, but video conferencing allows several people to talk face-to-face, like any normal meeting, but using a small camera, a computer and a network connection.

To use a video conferencing facility you would need:

- a digital video camera
- a microphone and speakers
- a computer with the appropriate software
- a link to the other computers via the Internet, cable or ISDN line.

The big advantage of video conferencing is that people don't need to spend many hours travelling to venues across the country to attend meetings. Meetings can be conducted from the comfort of your office or home, saving money as well as time. Unlike a telephone conversation, the people involved in a video conference can see *and* hear each other and, using the links, can send documents and data to each other electronically. This gives people the opportunity to have discussions and debates which would be much more time-consuming and difficult if it were done by phone or snail mail. It is very similar to the satellite links used on television programmes when people from different parts of the world contribute to topical debate. The quality of video conferencing isn't up to this standard just at the moment, but the software and hardware needed is improving all the time.

Internet browsers

To use the Internet you will need a program called a **browser**, such as Microsoft **Internet Explorer** or Netscape **Navigator**. A browser allows you to access the information stored on the **World Wide Web**, which may be words, pictures, music or videos.

In this section, the browser used is **Internet Explorer**, but many of the functions are similar in other browser programs.

The World Wide Web, or Web as it is often called, is made up of millions of documents called web pages which are stored on different computers all over the world. The browser software needed to look at web pages can help you to find, store, print and save some of the information you come across.

You start your browser by double clicking the **Internet Explorer** icon on your desktop, or by clicking the icon on the taskbar or in the programs menu. Your browser window will look similar to the screen shot shown below:

Internet Explorer

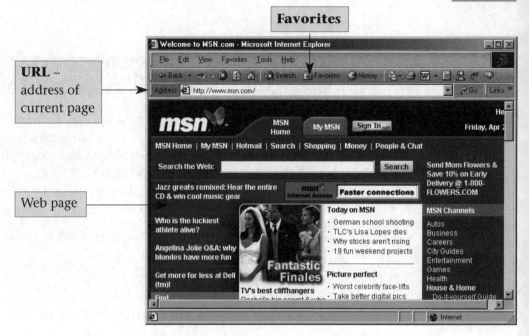

Figure 5.13 A browser window

Finding information

You can find information on the Web using your browser in several ways:

- If you know the **URL (Uniform Resource Locator)** – the address of the Web page – you can type this into the **Address** bar.
- You can use **hyperlinks** to take you to other pages on the Web. Hyperlinks are words or pictures which link pages on the Web and clicking on a hyperlink will take you to a new page.
- Using **search engines** can help you find information on specific topics (to help with your work, perhaps). Search engines are programs which will look through all the web pages to find ones which match your search. You type **keywords** about the subject you are interested in into the search box and the search engine does the rest!

Saving, printing and downloading information

When you have found the information you need, a browser will allow you to save it for future use. This can be quite helpful if you are **on-line** (connected to the Internet via your phone line, for example) paying call charges for each minute you are connected, as you can look at the information later when you have closed your connection to the Internet.

You can also save the addresses of some of the Web pages you use often to a **Favorites** (note the American spelling) folder. This helps you to find the page again very quickly by using the Favorites button on the toolbar and selecting the page you want.

You can print out documents from a web page using the **Print** button on the toolbar. This would be useful if it was a map giving directions for example, or some interesting information you wanted to show a friend at work.

Some of the resources on the Web can be **downloaded** directly onto your computer, such as video clips, music, programs or pictures.

E-commerce

You can buy an amazing variety of things on the Web, such as books, CDs, computer equipment, holidays, groceries; in fact the list is endless. This is called **electronic commerce** or **e-commerce**. It is a way of doing business on-line.

Many companies will advertise on the Web, and provide links to their lists of items for sale so that you can quickly find what you want. You can pay for your goods electronically, by entering your credit or debit card details. The pages where you would enter such sensitive information usually have special security features so that your information can't be misused.

These screen shots show how you could buy your favourite book on the Web:

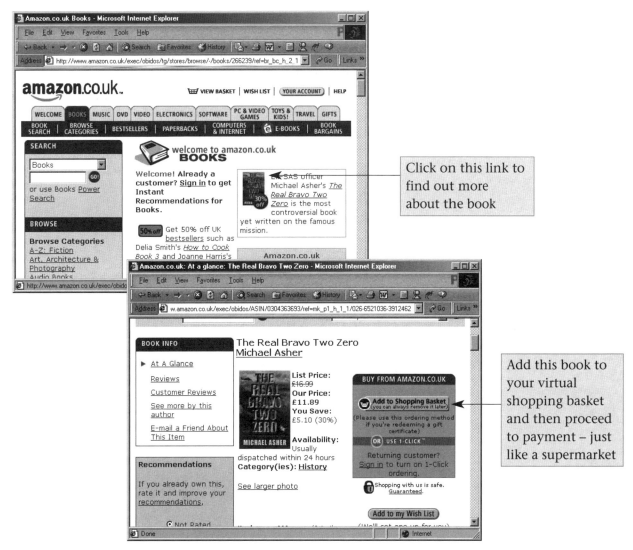

Figure 5.14 Buying a book on the Internet

Advantages and disadvantages of e-commerce

The advantages of e-commerce are:

- People who live in country areas can buy goods which are only available in stores in large cities.
- People can buy goods without leaving their home.
- Less trips to towns and shopping centres could mean less traffic congestion and less pollution.
- Shopping is quick and easy, with goods being delivered to your door, generating more jobs in delivery firms.

The disadvantages of e-commerce are:

- People could feel isolated and cut off without trips to shops where they meet other people.
- Walking round the shops is exercise; buying your goods without leaving home means less exercise which could lead to health problems.
- It could be seen as slightly risky giving out your credit card details over the Internet.
- Exchanging goods could be difficult.
- You can't 'try before you buy' when you buy goods over the Internet.
- There could be fewer shops, especially locally, which means that people without computers may not be able to get the goods they need.

→ Practise your skills 3

1 Open your e-mail program.

2 Enter the e-mail address of someone within your organisation who is aware that you will be sending this e-mail.

3 Enter **'Rover'** in the **Subject** box.

4 Enter this message: 'I'm attaching a file about my dog Rover – please will you let me know if it arrives safely.'

5 Attach the file **Rover** from your floppy disk.

6 **Send** the message. (If you are working off-line you will need to connect to your ISP.)

7 Close your e-mail program.

→ Practise your skills 4

1 Open your e-mail program.

2 Check to see if you have any new mail.

3 Read your new mail.

4 Print out a copy.

5 Close your e-mail program.

→ Practise your skills 5

1 Open your e-mail program.
2 Reply to the message you have received to thank the sender.
3 **Send** the message. (If you are working off-line you will need to connect to your ISP.)
4 Close your e-mail program.

→ Check your knowledge 2

1 To send e-mails to people you need to know:
   a their e-mail address
   b where they live
   c what their phone number is
   d what their home address is

2 A copy of any e-mail you send is placed in the:
   a Drafts folder
   b Deleted Items folder
   c Inbox folder
   d Sent folder

3 One example of a browser is:
   a Internet Searcher
   b Internet Explorer
   c Internet Surfer
   d Web Explorer

You will learn to

- Maintain a safe working environment for yourself and others
  - ☐ Use safe working practices at all times
  - ☐ Describe what elements and practices create a good working environment
  - ☐ Explain the importance of keeping fire doors and exits clear and unblocked
  - ☐ Use reporting procedures to report any hazards
  - ☐ Identify the health and safety precautions to adopt when using a computer
  - ☐ Identify injuries common in a bad working environment
  - ☐ Operate equipment according to suppliers, manufacturers and/ or workplace requirements
- Use and maintain equipment, materials and accessories to a safe standard
  - ☐ Identify cleaning procedures related to IT equipment

Maintain a safe environment

Using a computer can be interesting, challenging, fun and sometimes frustrating, but, like any piece of equipment you use at work or college, it is essential that you use it safely.

Safety is everyone's responsibility. To keep yourself and others safe you need to know the right rules and regulations. General health and safety in any working environment is governed by the **Health and Safety at Work Act 1974**. The safe use of computer equipment is covered by the **Health and Safety (Display Screen Equipment) Regulations 1992**.

Health and Safety at Work Act 1974

This Act gives details about employers' and employees' responsibilities in a working environment. It states quite clearly that you must not only be aware of your own safe working practices, but also look out for the safety of others. That is quite a responsibility, and one you need to bear in mind at all times when you are busy working.

Employers, too, have a responsibility to make sure they do what they can to provide you and your colleagues with a safe place to work and equipment that meets certain standards.

Many of your responsibilities are common sense. Would you leave a wire trailing over the floor where people might trip over it and end up having a nasty fall? The answer is – of course not! It's not just important to keep things like that in mind, but to also be aware of what to do when you notice something isn't quite right. Who do you inform about the trailing wire and how do you go about telling them?

Your first steps in making sure your work environment is safe are to:

- make sure you have read your organisation's health and safety procedures and practices
- remember the types of hazards which could arise
- find out the reporting procedures to get something done about any hazards you notice
- make sure your own work area is tidy and free from hazards.

Try it out!

- Find out about your organisation's health and safety policy.
- Find out how to report a hazard if you spot one.

Typical hazards in a workplace

- Drinks placed near a computer which could get knocked over – causing damage to the computer and a potential electrical hazard.
- Drinks spilt on a shiny floor could turn it into a skating rink.
- Moving heavy computer equipment around, especially if correct lifting techniques aren't used, could cause an injury or damage to equipment (if you dropped it onto your feet, it could do both!).
- Bags or other objects lying around on the floor, just waiting for someone to trip over.
- Drawers left open in a filing cabinet – this could result in a nasty injury if someone walks into them.
- Computer wires trailing over the floor (or any electrical wires for that matter!), which are a trip hazard.
- Computer cables stretched across an area to reach plug sockets – it could damage the cable and be a potential electrical hazard. All computer cables, especially power cables, should be safely secured at the back of the desk, and power points should be available nearby.
- Overloaded power points are dangerous and could be a fire hazard. All power points should be installed by a qualified electrician.
- Reaching up to high shelves without the right steps could cause a fall, and pull equipment down.
- Any frayed electrical cable is unsafe and would be an electrical hazard.
- Fire doors and exits blocked with any manner of objects would delay or prevent people escaping if a fire occurred. A frightening thought!

Try it out!

1 Turn the hazards mentioned above into a 'Do or Don't' list. Add any other hazards you can think of. There are eleven listed, can you make it more?

2 Spot the hazards in the picture below, and write them down. Note down what you would do to correct or report the problem.

3 You should also be able to recognise some of the common safety signs. See how many of the following signs you know and find out about any you are not sure of. How many can you spot around your workplace?

→ **Check your knowledge 1**

1 If you spot a hazard in your working environment, you should:
   a do nothing
   b tell your workmates
   c report it according to the organisation's reporting procedures
   d be careful to avoid the hazard

2 The safety of your colleagues is:
   a solely your responsibility
   b solely the responsibility of your employer or college
   c solely the responsibility of your workmates
   d everyone's responsibility

3 Which of the following is the odd one out?
   a Don't ever drink at work
   b Don't leave trailing wires
   c Don't leave filing cabinet drawers open
   d Don't overload power points

Health and Safety (Display Screen Equipment) Regulations 1992

This legislation gives details of the specific requirements of the employer in relation to employees working with VDUs (Visual Display Units).

These regulations are designed to make sure that:

- any risk to employees is identified and corrected
- all new workstations meet requirements laid down
- employees can take frequent breaks during the working day to reduce fatigue
- employees who use VDUs regularly have access to eye tests
- training in the use of equipment is given
- employees are provided with the appropriate information about their workstation.

Good practice when working with VDUs

There are good practices which you can adopt to make sure you minimise any risk to your health.

Your chair

- Your chair should be fully adjustable, and you should be able to adjust the height up and down so that you can move your legs freely under the desk.
- It should have an adjustable back so that you can get a comfortable, supporting position.
- Your arms should be horizontal when they rest on your keyboard and your eyes should be level with the top of the screen.

- You can see the correct posture for sitting at a workstation in the picture below.

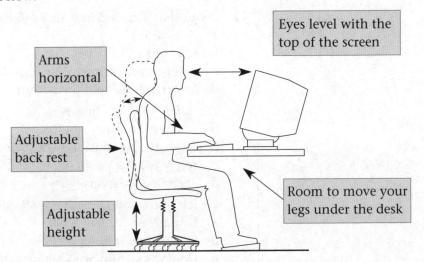

Arms horizontal

Eyes level with the top of the screen

Adjustable back rest

Adjustable height

Room to move your legs under the desk

- You may find a footpad to rest your feet on while you are at the computer could be more comfortable for you.

Your screen

- This should be fully adjustable so that your eyes are at the same height as the top of the screen.
- You may find a screen filter (a glass or mesh which fits over the screen and reduces glare) helps to reduce the glare of the screen.
- If your screen is badly focused, too bright, or appears to flicker, it's time to report the hazard (it could cause eyestrain) and get the screen looked at by a qualified technician.

Your keyboard

- Ensure your keyboard is at a comfortable height and that it is in the right position for you – you shouldn't have to stretch to reach the keys.
- You may find a wrist pad helps to relieve pressure.

Your mouse

- Use a mouse mat to help the mouse ball underneath run smoothly and make sure that you have enough space on your desk to move it around freely.
- If your arms or fingers become tired or painful when using the mouse, take a break and do something else for a while.

Lighting and ventilation

- Make sure that you are using your computer where you have plenty of light (although not directly on the screen, otherwise you won't be able to see what you're doing!) and that your workplace is well ventilated. Ventilation is especially important if you are using a laser printer which may produce ozone when printing (take care though – you don't want to open the windows too wide, a sudden gust could blow the window closed and shatter the glass).

You can find a great deal of information about health and safety from the Health & Safety Executive website at www.hse.gov.uk.

Try it out!

Work with a colleague to compare each other's positions with that in the diagram on page 108, as you each sit at your workstation. Are you both sitting correctly and minimising the risk of any injury or stress? What should you do if not?

Common injuries

You have now looked at a great deal of information about how you can make sure you work safely. You should bear all this in mind each time you sit at your computer.

Some of the common injuries that can occur at work are:

Repetitive strain injury (RSI)

This can be a very painful injury. It can develop when people carry out small, rapid, repetitive movements of the hands, wrists and fingers. It can sometimes be the result of incorrect posture when you use a keyboard or mouse, or perhaps it can result from not taking frequent breaks from your work. A wrist pad to rest on might be helpful if you find it uncomfortable to use your keyboard for long periods.

Eyestrain

This could be caused by constantly staring at a screen for long periods and straining your eyes. Taking frequent breaks away from the screen is essential to avoid this.

Using a screen filter and making sure there is adequate lighting could help reduce glare and therefore strain.

Some people may need a larger screen to make it easier for them to work.

All employees who use a VDU regularly are entitled to free eye tests, so they should take advantage of this.

If your image is not clear or the screen flickers, it is important to get it checked by a qualified technician. Making sure that you have a desktop colour scheme which is comfortable to look at for long periods may be better than a bright, contrasting scheme. You could try changing the display properties of your screen to find one that suits you (see Section 4 for information on how to do this). For some people changing the colour scheme can be very helpful in reducing glare.

Bad posture

We have looked at the correct posture to use when sitting at a workstation (see pages 107–108). This is important to avoid back strain, circulation problems or any other injuries which bad posture can cause. If you use a different chair from time to time, which has been used by colleagues, remember to adjust it to suit you – what suits a colleague might not be right for you!

Operating, maintaining and cleaning your equipment

Some of the golden rules for using and maintaining your equipment are:

- Check with the manufacturer's handbook to see what the correct procedures are.
- Don't 'have a go'. It may be tempting, especially if you think you can do it yourself. Always check the manufacturer's instructions and ask for advice if you are not sure.
- Always use the equipment according to the instructions. Whatever anyone might tell you, the CD-ROM drive drawer is *not* a coffee cup holder!
- Only clean the equipment with recommended or commercially packaged proprietary cleaning equipment and agents. It is important to keep your screen clean, and there are specially impregnated cloths for this purpose. Don't use the staff kitchen floor cloth!
- Take care when cleaning or maintaining equipment. Remember that you are dealing mainly with electrical appliances, and electricity is dangerous. Always check that the power is switched off before handling the appliances!
- Remember the health and safety rules at all times.

Some rules specifically for computers (although many of these apply to any equipment):

- Don't expose the computer to direct sunlight or place it near sources of heat such as radiators.
- Don't place the computer near magnetic fields.
- Don't expose your computer to rain or moisture.
- Don't spill water or any liquid on the computer.
- Don't subject the computer to heavy shocks and vibration.
- Don't expose the computer to dirt and dust.
- Never place objects on top of the computer.
- Never place the computer on an uneven surface.

These are all common sense rules, but just because they are it's sometimes easy to forget them!

Cleaning your equipment

Just like any piece of furniture or equipment, your computer can get a bit grubby, and you need to clean it. In doing so, remember that your computer is a delicate piece of equipment that needs special care and cleaning products! Here are ways to clean the various parts of your computer.

Screen

Like your TV, a computer screen builds up static electricity and this attracts lots of dust. There are many brands of anti-static cleaning cloths available for cleaning the screen – they are similar to the cloths you might use to clean your glasses (as in specs!). Cloths like these should be fine to remove dust, but if your screen is very grubby, with greasy finger marks for example, an anti-static damp 'wet wipe' would be best.

Remember:

Always check your equipment manual before doing your Spring cleaning!

Keyboard

A dust cover to place over your keyboard when you're not using it will help stop dust and dirt getting down into the spaces between the keys. To clean your keys, use a small, soft brush to sweep away any crumbs and debris, and follow this with a slightly damp (not wet!) lint-free cloth.

Mouse

However hard you try to keep your desktop clean, your mouse will pick up bits of dirt and fluff. Cleaning it out every now and then will help keep it running smoothly. If you find it starts to stick as you move it around the mouse mat – it's probably a good time to clean it!

If you turn the mouse over, the cover for the rolling ball is often a plastic disc which can be turned to let the mouse-ball drop into your hand. Clean the mouse-ball to take off any fluff sticking to it. Wipe inside the mouse with a clean, lint-free cloth and check that the rollers inside are also free of dirt. Replace the mouse-ball and secure the cover. Your mouse should now be able to roll around with total freedom!

There are products specifically designed to clean your mouse, and they can be purchased from most computer retailers.

Other peripherals

For these pieces of equipment you will need to refer to the appropriate manuals, which should give instructions on how and when they should be cleaned.

→ Check your knowledge 2

1 Under the Health and Safety (Display Screen Equipment) Regulations 1992, employers should ensure that:
   a employees who use VDUs regularly can have eye tests
   b employees only use new computers
   c employees don't have any training to use the equipment
   d employees don't take frequent breaks away from the computer

2 When working with VDUs, you should:
   a have you eyes level with the bottom of the screen
   b have a chair which will adjust for height only
   c have a chair with an adjustable back only
   d have your eyes level with the top of the screen

3 When using your computer mouse you should:
   a use a mouse mat
   b use a wrist rest
   c use a mouse with three buttons
   d use a mouse all the time without a break

4 A common injury when using the computer keyboard is:
   a repetitive keyboard injury (RKI)
   b repetitive typing injury (RTI)
   c repetitive strain injury (RSI)
   d repetitive wrist injury (RWI)

5 Which is the odd one out?
   You may need to get your screen looked at by a qualified technician if it:
   a flickers
   b has an unclear image
   c has a desktop colour scheme you don't like
   d is far too bright and can't be adjusted

6 When cleaning your computer equipment you should:
   a use a wet cloth
   b use a vacuum cleaner
   c use a scouring pad
   d use the product recommended in the manual

7 When using computer equipment you should:
   a keep liquids away from it as they might be spilt
   b make sure it's in a sunny spot
   c place your heavy file on top of the computer
   d place it near a magnetic source

Practice assignment

For this assignment you will need to have a document already set up. Ask your supervisor or tutor to prepare it for you.

Preparation

1 Create a document which contains the text:

MEMO

To: Roger Button

From: Dennis Jeeves

Re: Computer Specification

Following ouur discussions at the Partnership meeting last week regarding the purchase of two new computers for your branch office, I have pleasure in enclosing details of the machine we have recently purchased for our main office.

The computer specitcations of the machine are:

---

2 Save the document in an area available to the candidate with the filename COMPUTER SPECIFICATION.

Information for candidates

You must, at all times, observe all relevant health and safety precautions.

Time allowed: 2 hours

Introduction

This assignment is broken down into 4 parts:

1 A brief scenario is provided for candidates.
2 Task A requires candidates to identify the specification of a computer.
3 Task B requires candidates to open, edit and print files on a network.
4 Task C requires candidates to send an e-mail with attachment.

Scenario

You work for a firm of solicitors, Jeeves, Jeeves and Button, who have two offices in the North West of England. As a Personal Assistant to the senior partner, Dennis Jeeves, you work in the main office producing reports, leases, wills and other legal documents, as well as ordering some of the equipment used by the firm. Dennis has asked you to order some new computer equipment for one of the branches.

Task A

Dennis has asked you to find out some of the details about the specification of the computer you are currently using, as it is a new machine with a high specification and he wants you to order two more for the branch office.

1 What is the name of the operating system of your computer?

2 How much RAM does your computer have?

3 What is the processor type?

4 Enter this information into a word processing document and save it to a floppy disk with the filename MY SPECIFICATION.

Task B

Dennis has saved a document with the heading he requires with the filename COMPUTER SPECIFICATION. He wants you to add your information to the end of the document and e-mail it to the partner in the branch office for his comments. He asks you to check if you have access to this file, before you begin editing it. You follow this procedure:

1 Log on to the network.

2 Display the files to which you have access, produce a screen print and label it SCREENPRINT1.

3 As you do have access to the file named COMPUTER SPECIFICATION, select and access the application software. Open the file COMPUTER SPECIFICATION.

4 Firstly, spellcheck the document as Dennis hardly ever checks his documents. Correct the *two* errors.

5 Copy your file MY SPECIFICATION to your network directory and produce a screen print to show this. Label it SCREENPRINT2.

6 Open your file MY SPECIFICATION. Copy the text from the file MY SPECIFICATION into the file COMPUTER SPECIFICATION and paste under the existing text. Close the file MY SPECIFICATION.

7 Save the file as COMPSPEC. Produce a screen print to show this and label it SCREENPRINT3.

8 Use print preview to check the final layout. Produce a screen print and label it SCREENPRINT4.

9 After you have sent the file to the printer, you realise it is taking a long time to print. Check the print queue to see where your document is in the queue. Produce a screen print to show this and label it SCREENPRINT5.

10 The printer needs more paper. Add some more paper to the printer.

11 Switch the printer on, initiate a self test and print out a test page.

12 Print out a copy of the file COMPSPEC. Label this PRINTOUT1.

13 Dennis would like a copy of the file COMPSPEC on a floppy disk. Copy the file and produce a screen print to show this. Label it SCREENPRINT6.

14 Delete the files COMPUTER SPECIFICATION and MY SPECIFICATION from the network drive. Produce a screen print to show this. Label this SCREENPRINT7.

Task C

1 Use an e-mail software package to send the file COMSPEC as an attachment to the partner at the branch office at the address given to you by your supervisor or tutor. Use the following message:

'Attached is the specification for the new machine recently bought for the main office. Please let me have your views on whether this will be suitable for the two new machines agreed for your office.'

Produce a screen print showing the e-mail has been sent with attachment. Label it SCREENPRINT8.

2 Exit the application software program and return to the operating system environment.

3 Log off the network.

4 Note down reasons why it is important to have a virus checker installed on the network and updated regularly. Label your notes VIRUS CHECKER.

Multiple choice question test

1 PCs are sometimes referred to as a:
  a microcomputer
  b supercomputer
  c minicomputer
  d midicomputer

2 ROM is:
  a memory which is lost when the computer is switched off
  b volatile memory
  c memory which can't be altered
  d random access memory

3 An output device is a:
  a microphone
  b speaker
  c keyboard
  d scanner

4 To play music on your computer, which of the following parts is necessary?
  a CD-ROM
  b DVD-ROM
  c Sound card
  d Microphone

5 Dot matrix printers are used because they:
  a are cheaper
  b are quicker
  c will print sprocket-fed carbon copies
  d produce high quality printouts

6 You would use a modem to:
  a connect to the Internet
  b write an e-mail
  c load a program
  d save to the hard drive

7 You would print a test page to:
  a protect the environment
  b check the quality of the print
  c change a cartridge
  d set the paper size

8 The most common paper type used in printers is:
  a A4
  b A5
  c A3
  d A2

9 A VDU is a:
  a Vertical Display Unit
  b Visible Desktop Unit
  c Visual Display Unit
  d Virtual Disk Unit

10 A computer mouse is a:
  a pointing device
  b small furry animal
  c printer
  d graphics tablet

11 To check the spelling in your document you would use a:
  a word processor
  b spellchecker
  c spreadsheet
  d encryption

12 To produce a letter, you would use:
  a a word processing application
  b a spreadsheet application
  c an Internet connection
  d a database application

13 A GUI is a:
  a Graphics User Identity
  b Graphically Used Interlock
  c Graphical User Interface
  d General Users Icons

14 An operating system is used to:
  a produce your accounts
  b access other software on the computer
  c connect to the Internet
  d keep a record of customers

15 A virus checker should be:
  a replaced regularly
  b updated when you have a cold
  c never updated
  d updated regularly

16 You would use presentation software to:
  a produce slides
  b write a letter
  c perform calculations
  d produce a newsletter

17 To close down your computer you would:
   a unplug it at the mains
   b switch it off on the CPU
   c use the Start menu and select Shut Down
   d Use Ctrl + Alt + Del

18 To make sure that your documents are correct you should:
   a do a word count
   b use a virus checker
   c proofread and spellcheck
   d save the file regularly

19 An organisation holding personal information on a computer should make sure that:
   a they are checked by a virus checker
   b they are kept confidential
   c they are stored in a desk drawer
   d they are saved to a hard drive

20 You should save your work regularly to avoid:
   a memory loss
   b eyestrain
   c loss of work
   d encryption

21 How many bits are there in 10 bytes?
   a 8
   b 16
   c 40
   d 80

22 CD-ROM stands for:
   a Compact Disc Read Over Memory
   b Circular Disc Read Only Memory
   c Compact Disc Read Only Memory
   d Compact Drive Read Only Memory

23 To make sure you don't lose your data stored only on a disk you should:
   a password-protect the disk
   b copyright-protect the disk
   c make a backup copy of the disk
   d write-protect the disk

24 What kind of law might you break if you use an image produced by someone else without his or her permission?
   a health and safety
   b data protection
   c copyright
   d confidentiality

25 Which of the following shortcuts could you use to copy a file or folder?
   a Ctrl + V
   b Ctrl + X
   c Ctrl + Shift
   d Ctrl + C

26 A folder can contain:
   a files only
   b files or folders only
   c folders only
   d files and folders

27 To take a screen shot you would use the:
   a insert key
   b scroll lock key
   c the Ctrl and V keys together
   d the Print Scrn key

28 Someone could change the size of the fonts in the Display Properties dialogue box using the:
   a Background tab
   b Screen Saver tab
   c Appearance tab
   d Effects tab

29 To send an e-mail to your friend you would need:
   a a network connection
   b a browser
   c the town where he/she lives
   d a printer

30 You would log on to a network using:
   a your password only
   b your name only
   c your name and your password
   d any name only

31 Which is the odd one out?
   E-commerce means you can:
   a buy books on-line
   b book a holiday on-line
   c pay for goods by credit card
   d try before you buy

32 To open a file on a network you would:
   a select the file from a network drive
   b select the file from a floppy disk
   c select the file from the hard drive
   d select the file from a CD-ROM drive

33 To send a document via e-mail you would send it as an:
- **a** addition
- **b** extra
- **c** attachment
- **d** address

34 It is important to log off the network so that:
- **a** you can save your work
- **b** no-one else can access your data
- **c** you can back up your data
- **d** you can delete your work

35 To minimise the risk of eyestrain when using a computer, you should:
- **a** make sure there are no trailing wires
- **b** take regular breaks
- **c** use a screen saver
- **d** use a keyboard instead of a mouse

36 If you don't take a break after using your mouse or keyboard for long periods you could suffer from:
- **a** Repetitive Strain Injury (RSI)
- **b** Visual Disturbance Disorder (VDD)
- **c** Virus Infection (VI)
- **d** Poor Circulation Disorder (PCD)

37 It is important that fire exits are:
- **a** unmarked
- **b** unrestricted
- **c** covered
- **d** hidden

38 When working at a computer you should ensure that you have:
- **a** a monitor that flickers
- **b** an adjustable chair
- **c** all your files on the floor
- **d** light shining directly onto your screen

39 To maintain your computer you should:
- **a** wash it regularly with soap and water
- **b** place it in direct sunlight
- **c** place it near a magnetic field
- **d** read the accompanying manual

40 What does this safety sign indicate?
- **a** Fire exit
- **b** Canteen/Restaurant
- **c** Visitors' Exit
- **d** Dark Room

Solutions

Section 1 Getting started

Check your knowledge 1
1   c
2   a

Check your knowledge 2
1   b
2   d
3   c

Check your knowledge 3
1

2   a
3   d
4   b

Check your knowledge 4
1   b

Section 2 Moving on

Check your knowledge 1
1   b
2   b
3   a   ii
    b   iii
    c   i
    d   v
    e   iv
4   c
5   This will depend on the computer you are using.
    It may be Windows 95, 98, or ME

Check your knowledge 2
1   a, c, d, b
2   d
3   a
4   d
5   b

Section 3 Management skills

Check your knowledge 1
1 c
2 c
3 d
4 c
5 c
6 a

Check your knowledge 2
1 b
2 d
3 c
4 a   F
   b   T
   c   F
   d   F
   e   F
   f   T

Check your knowledge 3
1 b
2 d
3 a
4 c
5 a

Section 4 Working with windows

Check your knowledge 1
1 c
2 a
3 c

Check your knowledge 2
1 b
2 c

Check your knowledge 3
1 c
2 c
3 a

Section 5 Networking

Check your knowledge 1
1 b
2 d
3 b
4 b

Check your knowledge 2
1 a
2 d
3 b

Section 6 Safe working

Check your knowledge 1
1 c
2 d
3 a

Check your knowledge 2
1 a
2 d
3 a
4 c
5 c
6 d
7 a

Multiple choice question test

Answers

1	a	**11**	b	**21**	d	**31**	d
2	c	**12**	a	**22**	c	**32**	a
3	b	**13**	c	**23**	c	**33**	c
4	c	**14**	b	**24**	c	**34**	b
5	c	**15**	d	**25**	d	**35**	b
6	a	**16**	a	**26**	d	**36**	a
7	b	**17**	c	**27**	d	**37**	b
8	a	**18**	c	**28**	c	**38**	b
9	c	**19**	b	**29**	a	**39**	d
10	a	**20**	c	**30**	c	**40**	a